ADVENTURES IN THE SCREAM TRADE

Adventures in the
Scream Trade

SCENES *from an*

OPERATIC LIFE

Charles Long

MOUNTAIN LAKE PRESS

MOUNTAIN LAKE PARK, MARYLAND

Adventures in the Scream Trade:
Scenes from an Operatic Life
Copyright 2012 Charles Long
All Rights Reserved

Published in the
United States of America
by Mountain Lake Press
mountainlakepress.com

Library of Congress
Control Number: 2012934322
ISBN 978-0-9814773-4-3

Cover photograph © Joan Marcus
Design by Michael Hentges

Printed in the
United States of America

First Edition

To Pat and Marjorie Long,
Aldo and Eileen Di Tullio,
and Louise Williams

AUTHOR'S NOTE

I wrote *Adventures in the Scream Trade* as a series of
vignettes and anecdotes from my life as musician and
opera singer. A loosely woven autobiographical thread
ties together childhood musical experiences with my
ascent into opera and the denouement of my career.
I omitted unnecessary material to spare the reader
extraneous detail, to protect the privacy of others,
or to save for another day. *La brevità, gran pregio.*

—Charles Long, May 2012

Contents

PRELUDE TO A SCREAM   11

Andante Con Moto
Child Musician   13
The Language of Music   15
The Power of Song   17
Music School, an Experiment in Frustration   23
Summer Stock   26

Cantabile
New York   29
La Voce   33
Il Padrone   37
Church Jobs   38
Baritone Buddy   41
Early New York City Opera   45
Hong Kong   46
Back on Track   52
Italian Restaurants   53

Allegro Con Brio
My First AGMA Contract   57
It's Only *Rigoletto*   59
Managements   64
Louise   68
San Francisco   70
Houston   78

Cadenza

Auditions: Being Your Own Judge   84

NYCO Encore   88

Menotti and Barber   90

The Spoleto Festivals   92

Holland   102

Accelerando

When Opportunities Knock   110

It's Always *Rigoletto*   115

Sing, Herman! Sing!   117

Mental Preparation   121

Amsterdam versus Kennedy Center   124

The Smell of the Greasepaint   129

Under the Gun   132

The Conductor, *Il Primo Uomo*   136

Molto Vivace

Study, Study, Study!   140

Riding the Crest   143

Relationships: A Rocky Road   146

Manon Lescaut in Tulsa   153

Los Angeles   160

Galvani and Cincy and Sills, Oh My!   163

The Pearl Fishers in Milwaukee   166

Pagliacci in Beautiful Miami   168

And *I Puritani* at NYCO   170

Più Grave

The Glory of Victory, the Agony of Defeat   172

Postlude to a Scream: Perdition   178

Epilogue   180

The Road Taken   183

Postscript   185

GLOSSARY   186

ACKNOWLEDGMENTS   192

ADVENTURES IN THE SCREAM TRADE

ᕙ Prelude to a Scream

I sat at the grand piano, repeatedly banging out the same pitch for a tone-deaf student. It was dark and dank in the studio. Even the blanket around my shoulders couldn't keep out the numbing chill. The student seemed not to notice and fished for the pitch. He missed by a fourth. I sighed, smiled, and played it again.

I had come full circle—from aspiring student to international star to jaded teacher. I thought about how my parents had beseeched me to get a college degree so I would have something to "fall back on." Well, I had indeed fallen back—farther than I imagined possible. Those who can, do. Those who can't, teach.

I was awakened from my wistful reminiscence by another abrupt attempt at the pitch. It was a minor third too low this time. At least he was getting closer. I contemplated shooting him and feeding him to the dogs, thus putting an end to both our miseries. Surely no jury would convict me. A musician of my caliber couldn't be expected to endure this!

The realm of the classical musician is frequently perceived as a thing of ethereal, intangible beauty, distant and aloof, an untouchable museum piece, a world preserved by ectomorphic scholars in cobwebbed libraries, scrutinizing hieroglyphic scribbles called semi-demi-quavers, sextuplets, and *acciaccaturas*. Bullshit! This was hell on earth.

I looked at the pictures covering the walls of my studio: rows of 8x10, black-and-white glossies, the only legacy of a once-illustrious career. My mind wandered to a radio interview I had given years before. The interviewer was amused when I said that singing opera was little more than controlled screaming. I certainly felt like screaming now. I thought about my life and laughed bitterly.

The student looked at me aghast, perhaps thinking that I was laughing at him. Then, in a moment of inspiration, I stood and closed the piano.

"We're done. I can't do this anymore. The lesson is on me."

Without another word, I escorted him to the door, shook his hand, and watched him drive away. I felt a twinge of compassion, but not enough to call him back.

I walked from the foyer, through the living room, and out the sliding doors to the back deck. The sky was a relentless Seattle gray, and a light drizzle caressed the evergreen forest. This was as far removed from my fantasy of retirement as I could get. I'd always imagined myself on a beach with three Polynesian girls— one stirring my drink, one fanning me with a palm leaf, and the other ... oh well.

I've lived a fascinating life, I mused. Perhaps people would be interested to read about it. I should write a book. Yes, that's it! I'll write my story and I'll call it *Adventures in the Scream Trade*.

Andante Con Moto

Child Musician

Have you ever wondered why a person, against the admonitions of his parents, would decide to go into music as a career?

It is often the case that American musicians arrive at their early musical experiences through a school or church affiliation—not at all unlike the early careers of Bach, Handel, Vivaldi, and countless others. So it was with me and most of my colleagues. I began as a woodwind player at age nine and continued with a variety of instruments until I auditioned for music school at eighteen, as both oboist and singer.

I remember the first time I held an instrument in my hands: a shiny black B-flat clarinet, a cylinder of lacquered wood with glittering, silver keys. It was one of the most beautiful things I had ever seen. Nature had endowed me with an embouchure more appropriate for the woodwind instruments than for brass. Percussion didn't appeal to me, and, sadly, strings were not an option. There were no string programs in the schools nearby nor string players to teach them. Otherwise, I probably would have become a cellist.

I went home with the clarinet and a method book. My instructor expected me to decipher the first few pages by myself, but I didn't have the slightest clue how to decode those cryptic symbols.

At the first rehearsal the other kids started to play, while I sat there looking bewildered. The instructor, a wonderful man named Clarence Ebner, asked me why I wasn't playing.

"I don't know how to read music," I answered timidly.

This brought a hail of laughter from the others. Feeling like a dunce, I determined this would not happen again. I decided then and there to dedicate myself to this strange language of music.

I moved from clarinet to alto, tenor, and baritone sax. Then came flute, bassoon, and finally oboe. In this instrument I discovered an infinite beauty and more than enough repertory to keep me engaged for the rest of my life.

My oboe studies began with my first in a series of Italian mentors. Steve Romanelli played with the Pittsburgh Symphony. He also taught at Duquesne University and owned a music store nearby. He gave me lessons in exchange for my help around the store. After school, I worked the front desk, answered the phone, sold instrumental paraphernalia, and scheduled lessons for the several teachers. This was my first one-on-one experience with people who actually made music for a living. And what an eye-opener it was.

All the guys who taught in Steve's studio were active in the music scene in Pittsburgh and part of an elite subculture of professional musicians that exists in and around every major city. The larger the city, the larger this community. Pittsburgh at the time had a symphony with a modest season, an opera company that mounted a few productions a year, a well-established summer stock company, and various clubs and cabarets. Not much work, only enough for a handful of musicians. Thus, the pool of local professionals was small.

So there I was, learning my craft from these working artists. I was in heaven!

At fifteen, in a desire to round out my musical education, I began piano and voice lessons and participated in community plays and school musicals as both singer and conductor/arranger. As is true for so many people drawn to the arts, this was a way for me to stand out from the crowd.

Good thing; I was never much of a student. My scholastic record was a constant frustration to my highly academic parents, so these previously untapped artistic inclinations provided redemption from outcast status in a realm where grades and achievement were everything. Exhortations of "You better get good grades or you'll end up digging ditches!" rang in my ears. Only the music drowned them out.

❧ The Language of Music

As intimidating as it seems at first glance, musical notation is quite simple. Each of the eighty-eight keys on a standard piano has a unique location on what is called the Grand Staff. Each note represents a specific pitch, and where the notes are placed on the staff determines which key on the piano is played. The types of notes—whole, half, quarter, and so on—determine duration. One plays the pitch indicated, for the length of time indicated, and remains silent when encountering a rest. That's all there is to it.

Musical notation is perceived and translated differently by every musician, and it has been promulgated that math skills and musical skills are closely aligned. I don't know where this started, and though this may be the case in some circumstances, it is not, in my experience, the norm. I, for example, am almost anumeric. I have no mind for numbers and possess the least amount of math skills an adult can have and still function in the modern world. For example, I use my fingers for addition and subtraction. Yet I read music fluently.

Sight-readers can look at a piece of music and perform it, never having seen it before. This ability is highly prized among professionals, and few musicians reach professional status without having acquired it. Singers may attain successful careers without reading music, but all instrumentalists must sight-read with a high degree of proficiency. The goal is to comprehend a page of music as fluently as one would read a newspaper.

My first encounter with a great sight-reader was with a pianist friend in college, Jerry Jennings. For entertainment, some us would go to the library and search for the most difficult work we could find, often a symphonic reduction transcribed for piano or a full orchestra score. Then we would seek out Jerry, who was usually practicing diligently, a lock of black hair falling over his eyes. He would sigh at our approach and bark impatiently, "Okay, what is it now?"

"Play this," we implored, as we put the music in front of him.

He shook his head, peered over his glasses at the pages covered with black notation, and then … he played. We stood spellbound as he whisked through page after page, never pausing, never hesitating despite key changes and accidentals everywhere. A flurry of notes translated to music without preparation. It was miraculous!

Impressed by what I saw Jerry do, I dedicated myself to learning this ability at my own modest level. My sight-reading of vocal music was good—I had a church job that kept my skills well honed—but I wanted the pianistic facility as well. So I borrowed a church hymnal and religiously played at least five hymns a day, every day, never stopping for mistakes, never repeating a hymn.

Hymns are written in common keys, using the standard chord progressions and structure encountered in most basic music. As I worked my way through the hymnal, its predictable patterns and progressions burned themselves into my musical memory. By the time I had completed all six hundred and thirty-three pages, I had taken a giant leap in my music education. Pursuing the life of a musician requires an intimidating, ascetic level of commitment.

Today, more than forty years later, when I sit at the piano or scan an orchestra score, I still see those patterns that were etched into my brain. Like riding a bicycle, once you learn it, you never lose the skill.

The Power of Song

I vaguely remember singing in a boys' choir at a Methodist church in Butler, Pennsylvania. I can scarcely recall this experience, except that we wore little white robes. Costumes and a sense of theatrics appealed to me from an early age.

My next recollection of singing was in junior high. The music teacher paired students, requiring each duo to sing a Christmas carol while she accompanied. She matched me with a guy whose droning monotone was so overwhelming that I couldn't stay on pitch. I earned a D in music that semester. Incomprehensible! That comedy of errors effectively ended any further desire to sing for the next four years.

It's funny how minor traumas endure in your memory and build phobias that require a cathartic experience to overcome. Why are life's terrible events the ones that stay with us in such excruciating detail? Scientists say that adrenaline, along with repeated obsessive thoughts, are the fiends that burn trauma into your memory.

Restoring the gift of song was a monumental event. It also served as the impetus that would initiate one of the toughest decisions of my early life—my first crossroad. I had assumed I would follow the steps of my mentors: go to university, become a working musician, land a symphony gig, and leverage that into a college instructor position, maybe even a professorship. Not a bad life. If I were first-rate, I'd make a few recordings and go on tour occasionally. At least I'd be making music and thriving among my own kind.

But singing brought me attention, and I soon realized there were other options—very enticing options. There was the life of a musician, and there was a life in show business—on stage, the focus of attention, a key player, not just a pawn. I could be one of many in an orchestra, part of a privileged few indeed. Or, I could become one of the elite—a paragon.

It wasn't until I saw the operas *Cavalleria Rusticana* and *I Pagliacci* at Pittsburgh Opera that my aspirations finally took shape, funneling my efforts into the first phase of my career.

The tenor, James McCracken, was especially dynamic as Canio in *Pagliacci*. In the days leading up to opening night, local newspapers were filled with articles about him, and I read them all with great interest. I vividly remember an interview where the writer mentioned Mr. McCracken's yacht.

Yacht? Oh, my! This opera stuff is worth some serious investigation.

On opening night, I perched with my mother in the peanut gallery, where I sat mesmerized for two hours. At the end of the opera, McCracken stepped out for his curtain call, and the audience went berserk. I turned to my mother and said, "I'm going to be an opera singer."

Instead of having me measured for a straitjacket, she smiled that polite smile you give people when you want to humor their lunacy. But as the years passed, I'm sure she wished she'd called 911 and had me committed.

Twenty years after that performance, shortly before his death, I had the opportunity to sing twice with James McCracken, first in *Samson and Delilah* and then, ironically, *I Pagliacci*. He was one of the most delightful and gracious colleagues I've ever encountered.

One day after rehearsal, the cast went out to eat. When we finished our meal the waiter brought the bill and placed it in the center of the table. McCracken and I went for it simultaneously, each insisting that we be allowed to pick up the tab. Hoping to impress him with my financial success, I pulled out my American Express Gold Card and set it on the check. He smiled that beautiful Irish smile of his and trumped his Platinum card over mine. I let him pick up the bill.

The baritone singing Tonio in that same *Pagliacci* of my childhood was Sherrill Milnes, who shortly thereafter made a quick ascent to the throne, becoming the ruling American baritone of his era. Many years later, I had the rare opportunity to work with Milnes as well. I say rare, because singers of the same voice category infrequently get to know one another. This is partly because of competition, but practically, when singers perform the same parts their paths never cross, except in repertory companies where the operas are double-cast. Even then, you might pass in the hallway or otherwise know of each other, but you rarely associate.

More about Milnes later. Let's get back to the 1960s.

School was always a trial for me. I hated getting up in the morning, sitting in class repeating the same material year after year. Worst of all, I despised being forced to listen to some blowhard teacher pontificate on a subject that, even in my intellectual infancy, I knew I would never use again.

Curiosity is the key to learning. In my years in public school, I recall only two teachers who ever piqued mine. One taught literature and read Edgar Alan Poe's "The Tell-Tale Heart" aloud in class, followed by Shakespeare's *Macbeth*. I was hooked.

My second Muse of this period was Margaret Zook, a perky, attractive woman, recently graduated from music school, hired to teach high school chorus. By this point I had experimented with singing in my church choir and possessed a newly developed bass voice, courtesy of a blast of testosterone from Mother Nature. Even while consciously holding back, I could boom over the others in the chorus. This caught Margaret's attention, and she asked me to stay after class.

"You have quite a voice. Were you aware of that?" she queried.

Humble as ever, I replied, "Yes, I guess so. I've been singing a bit here and there…"

Did I mention that Margaret was very attractive and not too far from my age? And built? Needless to say, I jumped at any excuse to share her company.

She told me she was planning to mount the musical *South*

Pacific and wanted me to play the lead, Emile De Beque. I was flabbergasted and delighted. My mother had a recording of the soundtrack of the movie and another featuring the original Broadway cast. I listened to them incessantly, filling my mind's ear with the resonant tones of Giorgio Tozzi and Ezio Pinza.

During free class periods I worked on Emile's songs in the music room. Previously, I would have used these times to practice the oboe. But as I said, singing brought new temptations, and my mind was wandering farther away from my instrumental responsibilities. Anyway, there I was, seventeen years old, singing "Some Enchanted Evening," practicing a French dialect, and learning stagecraft—actions that would redirect my potential.

My success in *South Pacific* inalterably changed my life. My popularity soared. Cliques and social circles from which I'd been ostracized now sought my attention. I'd been blessed with a healthy ego, but now a unique self-confidence bourgeoned and with it a sense that I could use my newfound gifts to supersede the class valedictorian, achieving accolades and a future standard of living far beyond past expectations. It was intoxicating. I could thumb my nose at the authority figures who had chided me.

Ditch-digger, indeed!

Damned be their excoriating pleas for scholastic achievement. Some other voice was crying out to me with a greater passion. I didn't know if it was an inner state of grace, a trace genetic memory, or a psychotic episode. Whatever it was, it told me to be aware of my intuition, trust my gut-level instincts, and be my own judge. To exhaust all the clichés, I resolved to march to my own drummer, be the master of my fate, and the captain of my soul. The expectations of others were simply that—and that alone. It was my will and determination that mattered; nothing else.

That year I also sang King Melchior in a concert version of *Amahl and the Night Visitors.* My first opera. I didn't know much about the composer at the time or the fact that he was still active.

Nor could I have imagined this composer would play a part in one of the most wonderful and disastrous events of my yet-to-be career.

More about that later, too.

I was faced with a dilemma. I had spent years in endless hours of practice, honing my instrumental skills with the hope of becoming an oboist. But now my instincts were telling me this might not be the right move. I wrestled with all the possibilities. I thought of Steve Romanelli, who had engineered an oboe audition for me at Duquesne University. I had passed muster and been accepted.

My voice teacher at the time, though not as inspirational in her support, arranged a vocal audition for me at Carnegie Institute of Technology (now Carnegie Mellon University) with which she was affiliated. CIT, most notably a school for engineer types, also had a fine drama school. The music department was not far behind. I auditioned and was accepted, despite my less-than-stellar academic record.

I approached Steve and told him of my difficult dilemma. He stood silent for a moment and then said something that would help me make many decisions thereafter:

"Always follow your heart."

He put his hand on my shoulder, nodded, and that was it. Short, but profound. Inarguable.

Then my decision-making angst suddenly became irrelevant. An auto accident a few days before my eighteenth birthday sent me through the windshield, taking three of my front teeth with it. After months of dental work my permanent crowns were in place, but by that time my embouchure was gone. I faced the choice of excruciating months of practicing to get my chops back or pursuing a career as a singer.

Margaret Zook visited me on my birthday. I still lay in a hospital bed, looking like a war casualty. She gave me her score of

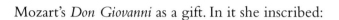

Mozart's *Don Giovanni* as a gift. In it she inscribed:

> Two roads diverged in a yellow wood,
> And sorry I could not travel both
> And be one traveler, long I stood
> And looked down one as far as I could
> To where it bent in the undergrowth,
>
> Then took the other, just as fair,
> And having perhaps the better claim,
> Because it was grassy and wanted wear;
> Though as for that the passing there
> Had worn them really about the same,
>
> And both that morning equally lay
> In leaves no step had trodden black.
> Oh, I kept the first for another day!
> Yet knowing how way leads on to way,
> I doubted if I should ever come back.
>
> I shall be telling this with a sigh
> Somewhere ages and ages hence:
> Two roads diverged in a wood, and I—
> I took the one less traveled by,
> And that has made all the difference.

The Road Not Taken, Mountain Interval
Robert Frost (1874–1963)

So, with good conscience, I chose the path less traveled. I still have that score and sometimes turn to those handwritten lines and contemplate what my life might have been, had I chosen the other road.

Music School, an Experiment in Frustration

Margaret Zook thought I needed more intensive guidance than she could provide, so in my senior year of high school she recommended another teacher. Every week I made a forty-mile round trip from my rural home, north of Pittsburgh, to the Shadyside part of the city and the studio of Beatrice Krebs.

Miss Krebs was an austere, zaftig woman with a dramatic demeanor—Brunhilde meets the Bride of Frankenstein. She had a shock of short black hair with outrageous white streaks that were swept back dramatically at the temples, making her appear as though she was standing in a wind tunnel. She'd made her career as an American mezzo-soprano, singing mostly in Germany and later settling into a plum teaching position at CIT.

During this period it was very difficult for home-grown singers to break into American opera companies. Around the time of World War II, many American opera houses had been seized by what was not so affectionately called the Austrian Mafia—musicians who had run from persecution in Europe. Predictably, in the snobbish American belief that "imported is better," these men assumed the directorships—or, more appropriately, dictatorships—of a substantial number of opera companies. Once they had them, they held on for life.

Unfortunately, with many of these men came a stern conviction that opera singers could only be trained in Europe, predominantly Germany. So it was that during the 1950s through the 1970s, if you wanted to sing opera, you were expected to relocate to Deutschland and work under a three-year "fest" contract. After completing this you were welcomed back to America, having gained experience largely unavailable here. But such experience was unavailable only because American opera directors wouldn't give singers a chance—a Catch-22.

A few years later, after I had moved to New York City, I

arranged an audition with Maestro Karp, the director of Pittsburgh Opera, during a visit to my hometown. I sang, he listened, and with a touch of an accent, he said to me, "You're good. It would be to my advantage to hire you, but I won't. Go to Germany for a few years, and we'll talk when you get back."

That was it. Short and sweet. But as determined as he was to shuffle me off to Germany, I was equally determined to stay in America.

I felt like Joe Turner in *Three Days of the Condor*. When it's suggested by Joubert that Turner has too many enemies in America and he should consider living abroad, Turner responds, "I was born in the United States … I miss it when I'm away too long."

Such were my sentiments about leaving my country. If I couldn't have a career here, I'd rather pursue something else. Regardless of the outcome, I was going to do it my way.

But back in 1968, buried as I was in classes at CIT that had nothing to do with furthering my career, I realized too late that a conservatory would have been a better route. A well-rounded education was fine, but it wasn't going to get me to the Metropolitan Opera. Not that I fared so well in my music classes, either. The academic environment held little appeal for me and even sparked a certain antagonism. When my curiosity was ignited, I was an insatiable learner, a fastidious self-educator. But the classroom, even the classroom of a prestigious college, felt like a prison.

I was even facing frustration in my vocal studies. Miss Krebs's understanding of the male voice was limited. While her sopranos and mezzos fared pretty well, most of her male students languished in a purgatory somewhere between competent and disastrous. I struggled with her for three years, even bringing recordings of great male singers to my lessons. I'd play them and say, "Listen. That's different from what you're telling me to do. I want to do *that!*"

She met my goals with startling resistance, but by the beginning of my junior year she relented. Agreeing that we had come as far as we could together, she introduced me to my second Italian influence, Lorenzo Malfatti. He was a wonderful singer with a light, fluid, Italianate sound, and he conveniently taught at a school nearby. At our first meeting I said to him, "Corelli, Warren, MacNeil, and Siepi do this 'covered' thing on the top, and their voices soar."

He smiled knowingly and said, "Of course they do. Let's begin."

It was marvelous. Within only a few lessons he converted me from bass to baritone and helped me confirm, once again, that my instincts were correct. I learned my first baritone aria, "Per Me Giunto," from Verdi's *Don Carlo*. In less than a month my voice blossomed, and all who heard acknowledged it. I was twenty years old, and things were finally starting to fall into place.

At the same time I was working with a wonderful coach at CIT named Rudolph Fellner. Rudy was a Jewish leprechaun who never stopped smiling. He had a *joie de vivre,* a quick wit, and a dazzling knowledge of opera and languages. Between the influence of Malfatti and Fellner, my vocal technique and artistry grew more in six months than in the previous six years. I realized that handpicking private teachers was the way to go—apprenticeships with skilled artisans. My patience with the academic environment was growing thin—and it with me. I knew that an exit, stage right, loomed just around the corner.

❧ Summer Stock

The previous year I had auditioned for Pittsburgh Civic Light Opera. At that time it was one of the largest summer-stock organizations in the country, playing in a huge, domed venue called the Civic Arena. They hired me on the spot, my first professional engagement under the auspices of one of the largest unions governing the show business industry—Actors Equity Association, aka "Equity."

Summer stock schedules are brutal. A trial by fire. If you survive with your voice and health intact at the end of an eight-week run, you probably have the makings of a real pro. The company rehearses one show during the morning and afternoon and performs the show that was rehearsed the week before at night. Eight shows a week, two on Saturday and Sunday, with the "dark night" on Monday. That summer I worked six twelve-hour days every week, with just enough time for lunch and dinner breaks. It was an eye-opening experience for a boy who had never worked a day in his life, and it created a personal work ethic (for show biz, at least) that was to serve me well in the future.

The company employed forty full-time singers and dancers to perform chorus and small parts. Most were hired in from New York. The rest came from Pittsburgh. We formed a tight community, though some distance existed initially between the home-towners and the New York troupe. Each day started with music rehearsals for the singers and class for the dancers. In the afternoon, with scores and scripts in hand, we'd stage the upcoming show.

This is where I first developed a taste for dancers. Observing these lithe, long-legged sirens stretching like cats in heat was mesmerizing. It was impossible to ignore a hard-bodied, young woman performing a split against the wall, spreading her legs apart farther than seemed humanly possible, as another adopted a provocative pose at the bar, preening in front of the mirror. Remarkably, there were no long lines of suitors for these tantalizing temptresses. It took me about a week to figure out why.

This was the summer I learned about the huge homosexual faction in musical theater. Of the twenty men hired by the company—ten singers and ten dancers—only four of us were straight. As the weeks passed, two more came out of the closet. But, hey, being the minority in such circumstances had its benefits. As my grandmother used to say when somebody didn't like what was being served for dinner, "More for the rest!"

In the ensemble during my second summer was a veteran performer named David Vosburgh. He was one of the nicest guys in the business and a short time later was lucky enough to play Roger Sherman in the original cast of *1776* on Broadway. David was openly and comfortably gay, as was his brother, of whom he said I reminded him. We hit it off and became friends. We bantered about each other's sexual preferences, and soon it became a running comedy routine. Remember the caution about never bending over to pick up a bar of soap in a prison shower? Well, sharing a dressing room with eighteen guys covered in pixy dust was a lot like that. You had to watch your back.

To make a statement about my heterosexuality, lest there be confusion about my inclinations, I made a big deal out of taping a Playboy pinup to the outside of my locker. This brought derisive smirks from the Boys in the Band and lots of jeering and taunting. All in good fun.

The following night I arrived to an unusually quiet dressing room. I knew something was amiss but initially didn't notice anything other than furtive glances from faces in mirrors. Then I saw them. Every locker and available wall surface was covered by gay pinup posters. A bevy of beefcake. A smorgasbord of schlong. I don't remember what I said, but I'm sure I blushed. I don't think I was even aware that gay pinups existed! I laughed and covered my eyes, which ignited squeals of laughter from bare-assed men dancing in the aisles. I was getting the third-class tour through the inner sanctum of one of the most steadfast subcultures of the biz. Sharing a dressing room with those guys was often more entertaining than the shows on stage. Homosexual men are not called "gay" for nothing.

In the orchestra were a few of my old friends from Steve Romanelli's music studio. I would often drop in to the musicians' lounge during intermission, where we'd swap stories about our various ends of the business. Sometimes the nostalgia ran thick. I missed hanging out with my pals—men who did manly deeds, chased women, got shit-faced at the local pub, and had a fist fight or two. But I'd made my choice, and there was no turning back. So, day after day, I waltzed my way through the land of the Sugar Plum Fairies, delighted that I had work.

I performed with a lot of talented luminaries those two summers: Patrice Munsel, Shirley Jones, Edie Adams, Bruce Yarnell, Chita Rivera, and many more. I did more than a dozen shows, lots of little roles, and developed a great love for musical theater. I met people who lived and worked in New York and was offered places to stay, should I decide to break out on my own. It was a training ground that bolstered my courage for the tough decisions ahead.

❧ *Cantabile*

❧ New York

After two wonderful summers of stock, some oratorio, and church work that provided a wealth of knowledge unattainable in a class-room, I followed my own advice and left for New York City on my twenty-first birthday. I ordered my first drink on my first plane ride—rites of passage to a new phase of my life.

I arrived to face a hostile environment, for which I was com-pletely unprepared. It was like walking into another dimension.

My plane landed at Kennedy Airport in the early evening. I took a bus to the East Side Airlines Terminal in Manhattan and a cab from there to the apartment where I would be staying with a girlfriend. Upon arriving, I paid the cab driver and included what I thought was an acceptable tip. As I stepped onto the sidewalk, he hissed an unintelligible slur in my direction, tossed the coins out the window, spat on them, and drove away.

That episode set the tone of my relationship with New York for the next fifteen years. Perhaps if I'd been raised in one of America's megalopolises, I might not have responded to the city as I did; but after the bucolic, rolling hills of western Pennsylvania, I found New York harsh, ugly, crowded, dirty, dangerous—and expensive. It was clear I wasn't in fly-over country anymore. I had arrived in the Big Apple, a label I soon came to believe should be more appropriately changed to the Rotten Apple.

Sadly, New York is the only city in the country where a young, aspiring musician can become a major player in the classical music industry. Manhattan Island alone has more opera companies, ballet troupes, orchestras, Broadway theaters, off-Broadway theaters, clubs, and cabarets than the rest of the eastern seaboard combined. The number of performances this theatrical activity generates is almost unimaginable.

There are good things, too: restaurants with exotic cuisines and neighborhoods with every conceivable culture; half-price tickets to theater, musicals, opera, and ballet; twenty-four-hour-a-day entertainment for every predilection—*if* you can afford it. As the saying goes, New York is a city that never sleeps, and it hides opportunity around every corner.

My first apartment in New York was on West 86th Street between Columbus and Amsterdam: a five floor walk-up with smelly carpets, a mini-refrigerator, leaky skylight, and half the cockroaches in Manhattan. Sounds like *Barefoot in the Park*, doesn't it? Wrong! This place had none of the charm of Neil Simon's play. The only good thing about it was the beautiful couple in the building behind me who lit candles every night and had sex by the window. I didn't have enough money for a TV, so I became a contented voyeur.

I was also soon treated to my first burglary, something almost every New Yorker experiences at one time or another. My few possessions evaporated in an instant, and questions of security became foremost in my mind. The police told me that hundreds of burglaries occurred in my precinct every day, so I should give up any hope of getting my things back. They suggested I buy new stuff instead, get better locks and, oh, by the way, "Welcome to New York!"

During this Mayor John Lindsay era, buses and subways were only twenty cents. As modest as that might seem, I often had to count my change to see if I would walk or take public transportation. Those years taught me some valuable lessons: Be grateful for what you have, and guard it well. The more you own, the more your stuff owns you. Travel light. Always sit facing the door with your back to a wall. Never carry a wallet or anything you would miss if it were stolen. Watch people's eyes. Predators give themselves away with that "lean and hungry" look. Such men are dangerous.

My fourth month in New York, I was riding a rented bicycle in Central Park with friends. As we passed into the northeast corner of the park, an area adjacent to 96th street, I noticed anxious expressions on my friends' faces. I didn't give it a second thought. I didn't know any better and rode merrily on my way.

As we rounded the northwest corner, they said, "Hey, we need to go faster." I was in better shape than they were, so I obliged, showing so much enthusiasm that I pulled far ahead of them while climbing a steep hill. I stopped, looked back, and waited as they pushed their bikes up the grade.

Next to them, a redheaded girl was walking a shiny new racing bike up the hill. When they were about fifty yards away from me, five black youths suddenly jumped out of the bushes and surrounded them. Knives and clubs appeared. Orders were shouted, but I was too far away to hear what they were saying. I started back down as one of the gang members clubbed the girl. Another stabbed her. A third mounted her bike and shot off down one of the paths. The others vanished into the woods as quickly as they had appeared. It all happened in the span of twenty seconds. The girl was crying and bleeding. She was in shock. We clustered around trying to help, ever watching the woods where the attackers had retreated.

Two guys on racers, who had witnessed the episode at a distance, approached and asked if she was all right. Then they quickly rode off after the guy who'd taken her bike. Within several minutes they returned to say he had disappeared into an alley on 116th street that was too dangerous to enter.

After a while, a police car drove by and stopped almost reluctantly. A wounded man, attacked in the same way less than half an hour earlier on the same stretch of road, languished in the back seat. His head was bleeding and his forearm was slashed. He had it wrapped in a makeshift bandage stained dark red. Our victim was woozy, but the stab wound to her abdomen was not deep and the bleeding had stopped. The police told us attacks like these were common on the north end of the park. Because the hill was so steep, gangs liked to hide in the bushes, waiting for an unwary rider to dismount. One would take the bike, while the others stayed to watch for more victims. Predators and prey, urban-style.

The girl became hysterical when she realized her wallet and keys were in her bike's saddlebag. She was terrified at the thought of those creatures having access to her apartment. The cops put her in the back and drove both victims to the emergency room. We wished them well and finished our ride, talking of nothing except our shocking experience.

The event traumatized me. I had seen something that might have happened in the Wild West or the English countryside a century ago, when highwaymen relieved travelers of their loot; Robin Hood and his Merry Men taking from the rich and giving to the poor. But the thieves I'd seen were not so merry, and there was nothing glamorous about what they'd done. It astonished me that, only blocks from million-dollar high-rises and the Plaza Hotel, denizens of the ghetto had brazenly attacked a helpless girl with as much emotion as I'd swat a fly.

Eventually the trauma passed, and I became nearly as desensitized to the rampant crime as any native New Yorker. I honed my survival skills and forced myself to refocus on the matter at hand: carving a small handhold in the music world of the Big Apple.

La Voce

A voice is a temperamental, idiosyncratic gift. Each one is unique. For this reason, singers have historically referred to their voices in the third person singular: "The Voice isn't really working today" or "The Voice of the great so-and-so…" The Voice is personified as if it has a mind of its own, and often, it does. As a barometer reacts to the slightest uptick in air pressure, so do weather changes, humidity, diet, sleep patterns, and air pollution perceptibly affect The Voice. The slightest change in a finely tuned voice is blatantly noticeable to the singer. Therefore, elaborate rituals are often followed to keep one's pipes in perfect homeostasis.

It was an unpopular philosophy while I was developing, yet it was always my contention that those who bloom early are probably the most fortunate. Like any extremely competitive business, the more youth one takes into the fray, the better. Show business requires an optimism and resiliency that is hard to muster beyond middle age. Performing and traveling all over the world call for enormous energy and physical strength. Don't let the stereotypes of rotund, pudgy-looking singers fool you into thinking that they're three-hundred-pound weaklings. Most performers who can maintain an international career over a span of years are true physical specimens, exuding robust health and great physical endurance.

Speaking of which, I'm frequently asked, "Why are opera singers such huge people?" Well, not all of us are. But great singers, like male porn stars, are well endowed at birth, and this bequest is not without its benefits. The stereotypical, big-framed singer who can make a mountain of sound is consistent with the laws of acoustics. Petite, coloratura sopranos usually have bell-like voices; bassos who stand like small trees generally make booming sounds to match; and full-throated tenors are regularly built like barrels with legs. So the stereotypes go, and all with scientifically justified reasons.

A good example would be to put a violin and a string bass in a hall and measure the decibels generated by the tones of each. The sheer size of the resonance chamber of the string bass creates a huge sounding board and thus a greater volume of sound. This is one of the reasons you see twenty-eight to thirty violins in an orchestra, compared with eight or ten string basses. Bigger instruments of the same family generate more tone. There may be exceptions to the rule, but it holds true most of the time.

I rarely exceeded a hundred and forty-five pounds and sometimes was mistaken for a dancer. One-forty-five might be fine for boxing at welterweight, but I was often perceived as too small for opera. Yet, I have a large-bore throat and a huge larynx, which helped me compensate for a smaller chest cavity. Though nature may have given some of my colleagues more formidable equipment, how they used those tools is another matter entirely. I made my impression with technique, beauty of tone, artistry, and considerable stage presence. Still, by operatic standards, I was thought to have only a medium-sized voice.

Acoustics also lend a hand in the phenomenon, as does the octave in which the instruments play. Small-but-high compensates for large-but-low. High pitches penetrate and carry more efficiently than lower tones, so there is often a tradeoff between size and pitch. Bassos Sam Ramey, Justino Diaz, and Norman Treigle were all exceptions to the rule, physically weighing far less than many of their gargantuan counterparts, yet with sufficient volume to compete on the international stage.

A personal example of this volume-to-frame equation happened during a production of *Il Marito Disperato* in Spoleto, where I was paired with the young Carol Vaness, a strapping girl from California, in one of her early performances. She was fully as tall as I and twice as wide. That's not to say she was overweight. She was veritably a "big-boned" gal, imposing in frame and stature. She'd sing a light phrase, barely using any energy at all, and it would slam out into the house. Singing the same phrase an octave lower, I would have to crank it up to seventy percent volume just to match her. The fact that she had an enormous resonance chamber and was singing at a higher pitch allowed her to make more sound with less energy.

Another California-bred soprano, Carol Neblett, was also a perfect example: tall, statuesque, large-boned, and capable of tremendous power.

But getting back to lifespan, many of the great singers of the past, from the mid-nineteenth century until the early part of the twentieth, made their debuts in leading roles at major opera houses while quite young. Some were still in their teens. Yet there was a strongly held conviction, much-espoused during my youth, that singers who started performing too early would ruin their voices. I remember preposterous stories about singers who supposedly did nothing but sing scales and *lieder*—art songs—until age thirty, thereafter bursting magically upon the music scene. I never met one, but such tales were rampant. I can't help wondering how they paid their rent, and what absolutely dreary personalities they must have been, living under a rock for almost half their lives.

I think what many proponents of the "wait-until-you're-middle-aged" philosophy saw was a natural demise of singers who sang early and sang hard. But I stress the word "natural." Other than the exceptional few, a singer's career, at the top of his or her game, is about twenty years. A singer is essentially an athlete who creates tone, rather than the observable feats we see from sports stars. Some interesting parallels in the sports world—where talent blossoms early and seems to fade quickly—give us insight into the life cycle of the singer as well.

Case in point: the great Puerto Rican welterweight boxing champion Wilfredo Benitez. He won his first crown at seventeen. Remarkable in every way, he took world championships in three different weight divisions by the time he was in his late twenties.

But then, to the astonishment of boxing fans, he started to slip. His speed, accuracy, and stamina began to wane, and overnight he looked like an old fighter as he was trounced by a young Sugar Ray Leonard.

Sports commentators made disparaging remarks about the eroding skills of a man so young, and no one could rationalize this premature deterioration. Explanations pointed to drugs, lifestyle, and brain damage, but investigations and medical tests provided no evidence. The boxing community was baffled.

Finally, an ex-fighter/commentator came up with the most astute assessment. He said, "Yes, Benitez is a young man—but he's an *old* fighter." He went on to explain that Benitez had been a professional much longer than most of his elders and had simply used up his physical prowess. It was not that he had less; rather, he had used it earlier.

Fans bemoaned the end of his championship reign and attributed tragic proportions to the event. I could never understand this. I preferred to view it in a more positive light. At thirty, with his fortune made and his financial security assured, he was free to pursue whatever new path he chose. What could be better?

Do I mean to insinuate that physical abilities have a limited and predestined life span? Perhaps, in general terms. An Italian tenor once told me he sincerely believed he had a limited number of high C's in his throat. He never sang them in rehearsal, convinced that every one used recklessly would bring him one note closer to the end of his career. You might laugh, as I did, but recent research on honeybees indicates workers are born with the ability to beat their wings only a predetermined number of times. When they've beat them all—they die.

We can't know if this has any relevance to human physiology. It could be that after a certain period of time involved in a single endeavor, some humans lose their competitive edge. But one thing is inarguable: The percentage of singers, dancers, and athletes who have remarkably long careers is quite small. Those who manage to stay near the top of their game for decades are the exception, not the rule. Specimens like Nolan Ryan, George Foreman, and Placido Domingo are icons of the superlative in their respective worlds.

My point is this: Sing whenever and whatever you can and while the talent is upon you. Don't leave it in the dressing room, and don't leave it unsung. You never know if you'll get another chance.

Il Padrone

Within a few weeks of my arrival in New York, I found a remarkable teacher and coach. Aldo Di Tullio, my third Italian mentor, reshaped and enhanced my concepts of aesthetics and musicality. From an Italian family in the Bronx, and originally from the Abruzzi region of Italy, he had been a pianist from an early age. Then, because of his love of the voice and his multilingual skills, he studied singing and became an accompanist and coach. Aldo had accompanied and mingled with practically every great singer of the fifties, sixties, and seventies, including his wife, Eileen, one of the most elegant singers of her time.

I could go on for chapters about my experiences with Aldo, but suffice it to say he became teacher, friend, father, and confessor to me. I'll never be able to repay him sufficiently for all the training and emotional support he gave me during those formative years. He took me into his family and loved me as one of his own. Here was a man who not only understood my dreams and could nurture and guide them but also had collaborated with those who had already achieved them.

My own family was not very demonstrative, so the exuberance of an ethnic family was quite appealing. A late-afternoon lesson often brought a dinner invitation. We'd sit and talk music. Sometimes, to make a musical point, Aldo would ask Eileen to come out of the kitchen—where she was making pasta, of course—to sing an aria or a Rachmaninoff song to Aldo's lush accompaniment. As though she'd been doing it since infancy, she'd fall into the music, spinning high notes with delicate precision. Then, without skipping a beat, she'd go back to the kitchen and prepare the sauce.

I went to Aldo's studio once a week and diligently studied music and language. He showed me how to perfect each tone, to give meaning to every word, to caress a phrase into a sublime musical expression. Everything I had learned up until then was child's play, meager preparation for the real work ahead: the art of singing.

Unlike the previous educational experiences in my life, now I was an eager and hungry student. My extraordinary apprenticeship with this man would forever influence my ideas about art, music, creativity, and life. Just as the sun radiated heat and light, the Di Tullios radiated music and joy. I spent some of my happiest moments basking in the warmth of their presence.

Now Aldo shares his benevolence with a new generation of young singers. At ninety-two, he still teaches and plays magnificently. As I write this, he is preparing one of the Mendelssohn piano concertos for an upcoming concert.

✌ Church Jobs

Throughout history, a traditional avenue of employment for musicians has been an affiliation with a church. Some of the most sublime music ever written is religious in nature, subsidized by some branch of the Christian Church. In fact, until Beethoven successfully promoted his own performances in the early part of the nineteenth century, very few composers achieved success without church commissions and subsidies from the aristocracy. Vivaldi and Handel dabbled in self-promotion, but the former died penniless and alone in a foreign land, and Handel struggled with various musical forms until his late-life success with *Messiah*.

The first paying job of my life was as the bass soloist of a quartet in a Presbyterian church in Pittsburgh. It was a dream job. It paid by the month and didn't require a midweek rehearsal, as most church gigs did. The quartet arrived at 8 a.m. Sunday and sight-read through the music. After breakfast we sang a one-hour service and then went home. I was only eighteen, singing with a soprano, mezzo, tenor, and organist who were ten to twenty years my seniors. It was an association I cherished for my two years at Carnegie Tech and an enviable first job.

When I arrived in New York City, I made it my priority to find a church job. The love interest in my life was a woman I'd met as a college freshman. She was a grad student on her way to Manhattan. We met again two years later in summer stock and started a romance. She was later to become my first wife. She'd been in New York for a while before I arrived and had already made some connections. After introducing me to an old classmate of hers who was a church organist, I landed a gig in the Scottish Presbyterian Church on 96th and Central Park West. There were higher-paying jobs, but most required the soloists to do an evening rehearsal to help the volunteer chorus members learn the music. This gig was a quartet, so just a brief read-through on the morning of the service was necessary. The job would provide my only economic stability for the next five years.

Singing for the Scots every Sunday was a practical asset in my life, but a friendship I made there became much more important. The soprano of the quartet, Liz Lamkin, was a remarkable woman who altered my views of femininity and opened my eyes to the virtue of diligence. She and her husband, both from Texas, were without question a beautiful couple. He was a tall, blonde, blue-eyed tenor who sang with the Metropolitan Opera Studio—an offshoot of the Met that did outreach shows in the New York City schools—and Liz was a dark-haired, exotic singer/actress. Pretty, self-assured, and talented, she had a bigger set of balls than any man I knew and was one of the most determined people I've ever met.

Liz and I developed one of the only satisfying platonic relationships of my life—not that I wouldn't have boned her if I'd gotten the chance. Like an Indian scout on patrol, Liz always had her ear to the ground, listening for hoof beats of the slightest opportunity. I, on the other hand, was raised an Irish Prince who led a charmed existence, never concerning myself with thoughts of promotion. When opportunities came to me, I casually took them, assuming that an endless stream would always flow my way.

The Big Apple was full of big fish from all the little ponds around the country. They migrated there to gobble up whatever they could, each one obsessed with fantasies of becoming a big fish in the Biggest Pond. Unless you were a clever and determined upstream swimmer, you would fall by the wayside, a mere statistic, your dream never realized.

At the crack of dawn, Liz would often leave a message on my phone machine:

"Get up, you sloth! I've arranged an audition for us at Such-&-Such Opera Company tonight at seven. I'll see you there."

Never one to look a gift horse in the mouth, I would haul my ass out of bed and go wherever she suggested.

Small companies were a wonderful training ground for singers who didn't take the European route and opted to stay in the United States. In my first five years in New York, I performed the title roles in *Don Giovanni*, *Macbeth*, and *Rigoletto*; followed by such juicy parts as Di Luna in *Trovatore*, Sharpless in *Madama Butterfly*, Marcello in *La Bohème*, Scarpia in *Tosca*, Michele in *Il Tabarro*, Tonio and Silvio in *Pagliacci*, Germont in *La Traviata,* and the villains in *The Tales of Hoffmann*. Although the largest fee I ever received was probably a hundred dollars, the experience was worth a thousand times that.

After countless auditions and rejections, Liz went on to become a member of the Metropolitan Opera Studio. At first they gave her little parts in this and that, but she had her eye focused on a greater prize. More than anything she wanted to sing Cio Cio San in the Studio's production of *Madama Butterfly*. While her voice was a bit light for the part, she had the stamina and acting ability to pull it off. She lobbied her way into the position of third cover.

Although Liz scheduled coachings and attended every rehearsal, writing copious notes in her score, her number-three position was so far down the food chain that her chances of actually singing the part were worse than Muhammad Ali's chances of beating George Foreman for the heavyweight title in Zaire. But you know what happened there.

Lo and Behold! A flu epidemic swept New York. The gal scheduled to sing Butterfly succumbed, as did her first cover. Remarkably, the second cover became indisposed as well, and Liz went on as Butterfly. She was extremely well received, and in appreciation—with some hard-assed negotiations on her part, no doubt—she was guaranteed more performances in future seasons. Her flawless preparation and patience had paid off. She was dauntless and eventually prevailed. Her example became a beacon for me. I emulated it, and it was to serve me well in the years to come.

Baritone Buddy

As I've mentioned, it's rare to make friends within your own voice category. But early in my audition cycle in New York, I met another baritone who would become a lifelong friend. John

McEvoy was a strapping, curly-haired Adonis I encountered at an audition. Somehow we struck up a conversation, and soon we were fast friends. In fact, thirty-five years after our first meeting, John was one of few to receive an early manuscript of this memoir.

John and I sang for each other on a daily basis. He had read numerous books on singing and brought a highly intellectual viewpoint to the process. He often quoted concepts from a book by Cornelius Reed—a controversial singing pedagogue—which prompted very heated discussions.

A few years after we met, John got a divorce and moved into the apartment upstairs from me and my wife. The three of us ate meals together, sang during the day, and watched TV at night. John and I even shared parts in an opera once, alternating between Silvio and Tonio in a production of *Pagliacci*.

We also shared enthusiasm for each other's successes. Most singers wish their competitors would die and burn in Hell. They visualize voodoo-doll likenesses of every singer who's making the ascent faster than they are and prick them daily with needles of envy. But when John was accepted at the Met Studio—except for a glimmer of jealousy—I was delighted for him. He had worked a lot in musical theater and had a splendid look and terrific voice. He was perfect for the Studio and deserved the opportunity.

One day, as I was preparing to drive upstate to sing Marcello in Puccini's *La Bohème* with a small touring company, the impresario called to ask if I knew someone who could sing Schaunard, the second baritone role in *Bohème*. The contracted guy had cancelled at the last minute. I told him to hold the phone and ran upstairs to ask John if he knew it. He did, and although he only knew the part in English, he agreed to perform.

The opera is in Italian, but it isn't uncommon under certain circumstances to hear an opera sung simultaneously in several different languages. Nobody cares, because most people can't understand what you're singing anyway. The promoters just needed somebody to wear the costume, act the part, and sing the right cues. So we packed up our stuff and headed out.

We arrived at a big auditorium in Podunk Junction somewhere in upstate New York, and all the usual suspects were in the cast. The clique of singers who worked these small companies was pretty exclusive. Once you found your niche, and the conductor and impresario liked you, it wasn't long before you became a regular. John was new to this group, but being a congenial guy he melded right in. Nobody cared he was singing in English. We'd never had a rehearsal, so everybody was winging it anyway.

Bohème, in my opinion, is one of the perfect operas. It's about two hours long, including intermissions, and each act is about twenty minutes. It begins with the characters of Rodolfo and Marcello onstage—one working on his play, the other adding brushstrokes to his painting. They sing for about ten pages before the philosopher, Colline, enters. The three of them sing for a few more minutes, and then Schaunard makes his grand entrance.

John entered and began singing. What came out of his mouth was neither English nor Italian but a combination of Italian-sounding nonsense syllables and lines from every Italian aria he knew, mixed with the contents of an Italian restaurant menu:

Di Provenza, cacciatore, rigatoni, pizza, cuore!

Yet he did it with such aplomb and confidence that nobody picked it up except the cast.

There's a show biz saying that goes, "If you make a mistake, make it big, and nobody will know the difference." That's exactly what happened. Throughout the show John sang whatever words came to mind. There were moments when it was all we could do to keep straight faces, which in a tragic love story like *Bohème* presents its challenges.

After the show when we were about to leave, an elderly gentleman approached us with congratulations. He looked directly at John and said, "Young man, you were wonderful! Such perfect Italian!" Our eyes met and we could hardly contain ourselves long enough to get to the car. We laughed all the way back to Manhattan.

John and I worked together only one more time; he was on the stage, and I was in the pit. But I'll tell you about that later.

Speaking of Puccini, I heard a wonderful story many years ago. I have no idea if it's true, but I've always liked it.

Puccini, one of the greatest of all opera composers—and my personal favorite—was traveling around Italy with a friend. They stopped for the night in a small village. His friend noticed a poster advertising a performance of Puccini's opera *Madama Butterfly,* to be performed that night.

Thinking it could be an amusing experience, Puccini's companion suggested they attend. This was a typical regional opera company. The orchestra was sparse and poorly prepared; the singers were local town folk, not the world-class performers both men were accustomed to hearing.

As the music began, Puccini's colleague cringed. The performance was excruciating, but he tried to hide his feelings. Puccini, meanwhile, sat in rapt attention until the love duet at the end of the first act, when he began to weep. His friend, feeling responsible for putting this great composer through the painful experience of hearing his work butchered, said, "Giacomo, I'm so sorry. I know this must be dreadful for you."

Puccini turned to him, smiling through his tears, and said, "No. I'm crying because it's *so* beautiful."

Despite the conditions of the performance, Puccini was able to wipe away the tarnish and experience the treasure beneath. What a wonderful way to perceive the world. If only we could all do this, how much happier we'd be.

Early New York City Opera

During my first six months in New York I worked a few "real" jobs and quickly realized I was never cut out for a nine-to-five existence. Through a series of introductions, I received an opportunity to sing for Chris Nance, the chorus master at New York City Opera. I sang "Avant de Quitter Ces Lieux" from *Faust*, and he hired me on the spot to sing Extra Chorus in the new production of *Mefistofele*.

This gig not only provided deliverance from a dreary office job at the time, but as a member of the company, it also allowed me to see as many performances as I wished, free of charge. Few evenings passed when I wasn't standing in the wings or seated in the company box, watching the rising young artists of the day, including Domingo, Carreras, Sills, and the remarkable basso Norman Treigle. These performances were enhanced by the efforts of a throng of gifted stage directors, conductors, makeup artists, and designers too numerous to mention.

It was a Golden Age at NYCO, as we called it, and I was delighted to play a small part. I stayed there for about two years, as did my wife. We earned just enough money to cover the bills and pay for lessons, but it didn't matter. I had a little slice of Heaven.

As delighted as I was, it was difficult working as a chorus member. Mine was not an ego that dealt easily with being one of many, but I realized it was a means to an end and a unique kind of apprenticeship. I sublimated my alpha-male tendencies, did my job, and gleaned whatever I could from the opportunity. I knew I was not ready to share the stage with most of the solo artists, but I knew, as surely as the sun would rise in the east, I was on the brink of my own sunrise, and one day I would be on that stage in an entirely different capacity.

❧ Hong Kong

I don't remember how I came to meet him, but Richard Barry was an odd man. He had one of those 'dos with the hair parted at the back and combed forward to cover his bald spot. He owned a four-story brownstone on the upper Westside and lived with his male companion on the top floor while renting the lower levels. Richard was the director and leading tenor of his own opera company, and though he was fluent in Italian, he had a painful American accent. As an actor he was outlandish, as a director he was obnoxious, and as a singer he was shockingly dreadful—a triple threat in reverse.

Despite his lack of talent, this man loved opera and had a heart of gold. He engaged me and my wife to sing opera excerpts in out-of-the-way places. One such tour took us to the hills of Appalachia, one of the most depressing places I've ever been. The audience, riddled with poverty and defeat, was straight out of *Deliverance*. The show was in West Virginia, only about a hundred miles from where I grew up, but it was nothing like home, and I couldn't wait to leave.

Because Richard was such a nice man and, more important, because his checks never bounced, we worked for him frequently. One day he announced he had booked a cultural exchange tour to Hong Kong and Southeast Asia through a Chinese friend, and he wanted us to come along. The deal included a round-trip ticket to Kuala Lumpur, with stops at other exotic ports of call, so we thought, why not? We might never get a chance to see this part of the world again. We had nothing to lose.

The only problem was our cats. We had acquired two from a gal who was so overrun with them they had turned feral and trashed her apartment. We took a male and a female, which meant within a few months we had three more, two of which retained the genetic traits of the mother and were too undomesticated to handle. We shipped them off to my in-laws in North Carolina. They were dog people but relented, since they had a large back yard in a mild climate. We kept the third of the litter, which we named Aldo, because of the white streak running up the middle of his head like his namesake.

We found someone to sublet our apartment and take care of the cats. Once everything was arranged, sometime in November, we boarded a flight to Hong Kong via Honolulu and Tokyo.

Even today, flying to the Far East is a daunting experience, but in the early seventies it was grueling times ten. Traveling for thirty-six hours with long stopovers, we finally arrived. A bus took us to the Chinese section of Hong Kong Island where we were deposited in a contemporary hotel overlooking a soccer field.

The next day we marched *en masse* to a large, European-style theater and began rehearsals for an opening less than a week later. The show consisted of scenes from *Otello, Trovatore, Fledermaus,* and *Traviata,* along with numerous mix-and-match arias and duets. There was no budget for an orchestra, so we brought our own pianist, Terry Lusk, from San Francisco Opera. The total troupe was eleven: four sopranos, two tenors, two baritones, two ballet dancers, and Terry. We were upbeat and enthusiastic about singing in such a beautiful theater—until we got free tickets to the closing show of the production preceding us.

It was a glitzy, Japanese, Broadway-style production, with spectacular costumes and lavish, prerecorded music played over a modern sound system. The place was packed. An all-girl cast played all the parts, and they were wonderful. It was strobe lights and beautiful Japanese girls dancing to raucous up-tempo music. Above all, it was everything we were not.

At intermission, Terry had an odd smile on his face. When I asked him what he was thinking, he said, "We're in big trouble."

He didn't know the half of it. Not only would it be difficult to compete with a show like that, but the tickets for our performance were priced at more than a month's salary for the average Hong Kong resident. Opera has always been a rarified art form, and I had assumed we were being subsidized by the Hong Kong government. But such was not the case. Richard's friend was not that well connected. If we couldn't fill the house, the tour would come to an abrupt end.

Opening night was dismal. We stood on a huge stage, two or three at a time, singing long-winded duets with only a piano accompaniment, which we could hardly hear, because the piano was buried in the orchestra pit. The rudimentary lighting—not much more than work lights—illuminated a few props, tables, and chairs strewn over an almost empty stage. So much for our set.

The house was practically empty, too, with perhaps a hundred patrons scattered throughout the orchestra section. The two ballet dancers broke the monotony of the performance with a *pas de deux* accompanied by some pre-taped orchestral music, but without somebody to run the sound system even that seemed tacky.

There was dead silence in the communal dressing room after the show. We sat in front of our mirrors, slowly removing makeup and costumes, lost in our thoughts. Richard walked in from his private dressing room, seemingly oblivious to the humiliating disaster we had just endured. He was beaming. He went on and on about the performance and the rest of tour. We stared at each other. *Has this guy lost his marbles?*

Then a gal named Rona, the group comedian, thankfully said something about the Chinese being good sleepers, since we'd heard more snores than applause during the show. Everybody laughed, except Richard. Without another word, he turned around and walked out. The rest of us packed up our things and headed for the hotel bar to get smashed.

The next day the reviews—if you could call them that—came out. More like obituaries, they listed the names of those who had died with egg on their faces the evening before. By lunchtime, we got the word that the show had closed. There would be no Singapore, no Malaysia, and no more exotic ports of call. We were halfway around the world with nothing but return-trip tickets and a few worthless Hong Kong dollars in our pockets. Some of us had given up gigs in New York to come on this tour, and all of us had left friends and family for the holidays. We pondered our options.

Then things moved quickly. A representative from the city government—still British at the time—got word of our predicament and arranged for us to split some shows with a Chinese Opera troupe. We agreed, and it was to become the most fascinating part of the trip.

The performances took place in parks around the city. We shared a dressing room with singers from another culture, communicating via translator and lots of hand signals and body language. We watched in fascination as they applied their intricate, multi-layered makeup and practiced twirling fans, swords, and canes. Chinese Opera is highly stylized and athletic, with grand gestures and lots of leaping and hopping. Nothing about it is dull. Even their weird, whiny, sing-songy voices became appealing after a while.

Like the all-girl Japanese show, Chinese Opera was a startling contrast to our comparatively stilted art form. We feared it was going to be a tough sell to the crowds who had come to the parks for a free evening's entertainment. But we actually fared better there than at the theater. The crowds loved our loud high notes, and they'd scream and clap in appreciation when we sang at the top of our voices. After our first performance, we made huge cuts, leaving only the flashiest sections in place.

Know your audience.

We usually performed the first half of the show, and then the Chinese company took their turn. They had an orchestra of about a dozen musicians, playing an assortment of odd instruments.

One night, I looked over the shoulder of a musician who was drawing a bow across something vaguely resembling a one-stringed cello, constructed of what appeared to be a broom and a cigar box. The notation was unintelligible. Talk about hieroglyphic scribbles! It was like no music I had ever seen. From what I was told later, it was probably the lyrics, not the music, since there is no formal notation or tablature for Chinese music. What they played, they played from memory. And they played with gusto.

After a couple of weeks, when it looked like a return home was inevitable, we received yet another reprieve. An American who owned a set of nightclubs had read our reviews and asked if we'd consider performing a Thanksgiving/Christmas show. He offered to pick up our hotel bills and give us each a small stipend. After a vote, we decided to do it. None of us was ready to head back to a bleak winter in New York with no job prospects. That night, we went to the club on Hong Kong Island. All of us, except Richard, had done musical theater, so everybody had suggestions. The club owner gave us a few days to find some music and come up with a show.

The next day I went to a music store and bought sheet music, pens, and a stack of manuscript paper. For three days, I sat writing arrangements, silently thanking my parents for all my music lessons and congratulating myself for having learned all those instruments in high school. I kept it simple, with songs and duets culminating in a big Christmas medley finale.

One of the girls had done a lot of Broadway and, with the help of the dancers, created some loose choreography. While I scribbled, the others choreographed and rehearsed. The force-marched creativity was wonderfully exhilarating.

There was no fanfare to our second opening in Hong Kong. Nor was there time to rehearse with the band. We threw together some of the costumes from our dead show and dressed it up with odds and ends, courtesy of a few bucks from the club owner.

Terry took the pianist's place for our set, while I passed out the parts I'd painstakingly written. After I handed him his part, the Korean tenor-sax player looked at me like I'd presented him with a ransom note. He and the guy next to him compared charts and shared a laugh. I thought, *Oh, fuck, here we go!*

Then the curtain rose, the stage rolled out onto the dance floor, and the band started to play. My God, they were good! They took the sparsely written parts I had given them and made the music their own, improvising their way through the charts. Terry sat there looking at his pages in confusion, then threw his hands up and let the Korean pianist have his seat back.

There were two shows every night, one at the King's Club in Hong Kong from ten to eleven-thirty, and the other at the Queen's Club in Kowloon from midnight to one-thirty. We had just enough time between shows to catch the ferry and a taxi to the other club. The two ballet dancers sang and danced, too, so we were able to form a rotation that gave everybody one night off every week. This continued though the middle of December, and I have to admit it was fun.

A city like Hong Kong can have an interesting effect on people. Some of us felt it could be a place to start over. We met people at the local TV station through the publicity we'd received and quickly became part of the expatriate community. As mini-celebrities, we were invited onto TV talk shows, and one of our troupe was even contemplating a new career in television. Another had been offered a job teaching English. Hong Kong was an open door, and it was exciting to consider leaving the Western world behind to make the most of this opportunity. As one of our new friends told us, the Chinese symbol for crisis and opportunity is the same character.

It was winter in New York, but we were swimming in the languid waters of the South China Sea by day and singing in a swanky nightclub by night. Ten classically trained voices singing

"Tonight" from *West Side Story* was something this crowd didn't hear every day, and they recognized it as something special. The affluent inhabitants of Hong Kong, both Caucasian and Asian, frequented the clubs, and hobnobbing with this crowd became a vicarious peek into another world.

But all good things must come to an end, and a few days before Christmas we headed our separate ways, promising to meet for lunch in New York. I never saw most of them again.

Back on Track

On a miserable, cold day in January, my wife and I crammed our three hundred pounds of luggage into a cab at Kennedy Airport and rode back to our apartment on West 72nd Street. With some reluctance, we returned to our lives.

Within a few weeks things were back to normal. She reclaimed her church job—mine had been lost to a replacement—and we resumed the incessant job hunt.

Almost immediately, I noticed my nose was stuffed and my eyes were itchy when I awoke each morning. Assuming this condition was a temporary reaction to the sudden change in environment, I ignored it. I used eye drops and a little nose spray. Over the ensuing months, the stuffed nose developed a constant postnasal drip, and my eyes became so red and inflamed that wearing my contact lenses became impossible.

A drip going down the back of the throat is one of the worst things for The Voice. Mucus collects and phlegm clings to the vocal cords. In reaction, the cords become swollen and irritated. I started to have difficulty singing, and whatever was affecting me became chronic: non-stop sneezing, hoarseness, and near blindness from swollen eyes.

My doctor peered up my nose and told me I had the classic,

gray nasal tissue of an allergic person. A battery of skin tests determined that I was highly allergic to cats, dust mites, and certain grasses. This astonished me. I never had allergies as a child and my health had always been magnificent, to say the least. He said it was rare, but sometimes people developed allergies as adults even though they displayed no such indications as children. He went on to say that traveling to other parts of the world can create new sensitivities. We had been in Asia for three months, and apparently my body chemistry had changed.

The bottom line was that I had to rid my environment of the offending contaminants and start a series of expensive injections.

Our three remaining cats had become beloved pets. The thought of exiling them to the wilds of North Carolina was emotionally agonizing, but it had to be done. With heavy hearts we shipped them off to what was probably a far better life. We scoured the apartment, and I started my injections. In three months, the symptoms diminished, but I never quite returned to normal. Changes in weather and the seasons brought unpredictable results. Also, the fluid-laden tissue in my sinuses had become a welcome breeding-ground for rhino viruses, rendering me extremely susceptible to colds.

I experimented with a range of over-the-counter drugs and a barrage of prescription medications and found a way to maintain balance. But if I came within half a mile of somebody with a cold, I would likely catch it. This was the first sign of an Achilles' heel.

Italian Restaurants

The Italian eateries in and around New York served as another mainstay in a singer's economy. Margarita and Bianchi's in the West Village was one such restaurant. Only a few blocks from where *The Fantasticks* played a forty-two-year run, M&B was an elegant little establishment known for its authentic Italian cuisine and live opera from six until midnight every evening.

As one in the M&B stable of singers, I was given dinner when I arrived, supper before I left, and twenty-five dollars in cash. A mix-and-match of three voices performed on any given night, so we were all highly motivated to experiment with repertory. Every week I learned something new. Before attempting an untried piece on an audition, I tested it at M&B. I gauged audience response with my internal applause meter. If it felt good and the crowd responded, it was probably safe to use, and repeating it night after night seated the piece. This is what singers call "working something into the voice." Normally, one pays a coach for this; at M&B, they were paying me.

Ephron Puig, a Cuban tenor who had escaped Castro's regime by floating to Florida on a raft, was a regular at M&B, and we soon became amigos. Ephron distinguished himself by doing the best Marlon Brando impersonation I've ever seen. He had a solid voice that rarely missed, and over the years we sang every tenor/baritone duet in the repertory.

I also became acquainted with a denizen of one of New York's most fascinating underground cultures. Ernesto Fornasiero had come to the United States twenty-five years earlier. He lived in the Ansonia Hotel and still spoke very broken English. He managed to avoid any problem with the language by moving back and forth between the Ansonia and other isolated Italian communities throughout the area, rarely stopping in between. He could decipher the bus and subway routes but otherwise never used English. Ernesto was a marvelous pianist. He knew all the Italian stuff from memory and could transpose to any key at sight.

Some of us at M&B were doubling at another Italian restaurant called Sergio's, about an hour out of the city. We'd meet at the Ansonia Hotel and drive upstate. The gig was pretty much the same as M&B, but because of the commute, it paid a little more.

The great thing about this place was the presence of one particular family that patronized it. You could always spot them at one of the large tables in the corner—the men exquisitely dressed, the women stunning if a bit garish. Some big guys, not so nicely attired, sat strategically placed at all the entrances. This was a big music-loving group, and they made frequent requests. Each time a request was honored, the distinguished gentleman at the head of the table sent one of the ladies to the tip bowl on the piano with a hundred dollar bill. At the end of the evening we split the tips. One night, I left with enough cash to pay the month's rent and a bit extra.

Unfortunately, a tendency to become temperamental ended the party at Sergio's for me. It happened one night when the place was packed and, with all the noise and confusion, the microphones had been switched off. In such a large establishment with cubicles and partially walled-off rooms, it was difficult to be heard without the mics. I got up and started to sing, but the background noise was so raucous that I couldn't hear the piano or even my own voice. I stopped abruptly, strode back to the singers' table and sat down. Sergio approached to ask why I had stopped. I explained my predicament and told him that I'd be happy to continue once the mics had been turned on again.

You'd have thought I had called his mother a *puttana* (in genteel terms, a woman of the evening). He turned red and told me to follow him outside. It had been a while since I'd done any boxing, and I wasn't anxious to start again in a dark parking lot with this *goombah* and his cronies. Nevertheless, I began ratcheting myself up for a toe-to-toe brawl.

We were about the same height, but he was unquestionably heavier, so I figured I could jab and move until he got tired. I wondered whether he was a righty or a southpaw, but it probably wasn't going to make any difference in a street fight.

Once outside, this guy started into a routine reminiscent of

Joe Pesci in *Goodfellas*. Snarling and with teeth gnashing, he let me know I had disrespected him, and I was lucky he didn't break my legs. It escalated from there. I kept my distance, circling to my left, waiting for him to throw the first punch. But it never came. Mid-roar, he stopped, snorted like a bull, and went back inside. I waited, contemplating my options.

A minute later he reappeared at the door. "I don't ever want to see you here again," he said, as he threw my music onto the pavement.

I sat in the car for two hours until my colleagues finished. As we drove back to the city the soprano said to me, "You know, the funny thing is, as soon as he came back in, he turned the mic on!"

As Don Carlo in Verdi's *La Forza Del Destino*,
contemplating his fate during his aria "Urna Fatale"

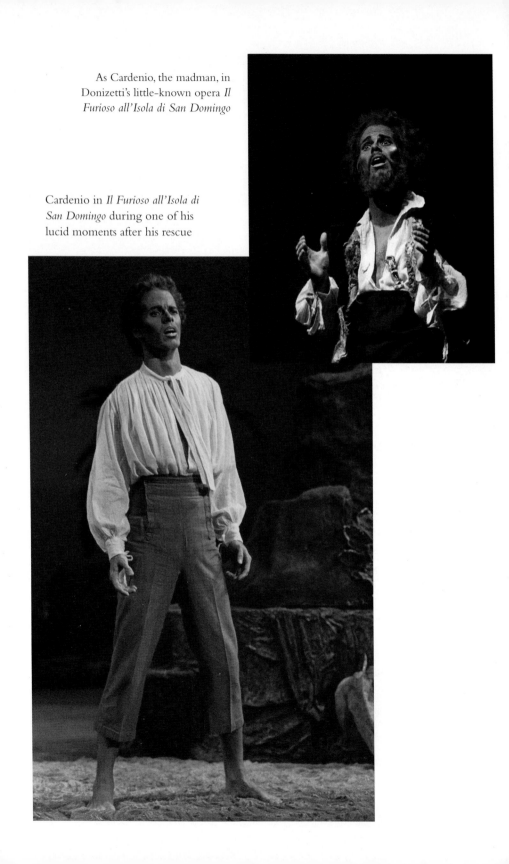

As Cardenio, the madman, in Donizetti's little-known opera *Il Furioso all'Isola di San Domingo*

Cardenio in *Il Furioso all'Isola di San Domingo* during one of his lucid moments after his rescue

Jack Rance, gunslinger and Sheriff
of a small Sierra mining town in
Puccini's *La Fanciulla Del West*

Photographs copyright Beth Bergman

In a jealous rage, Jack Rance
searches Minnie's cabin for his nemesis
in *La Fanciulla Del West*

As Cascart, singing "Zaza, Piccola Zingara"
to soprano Patricia Craig in Cincinnati Opera's
revival of Leoncavallo's *Zaza*

As the deformed and vengeful Tonio
in Leoncavallo's *I Pagliacci*

Tonio attempts to charm
Nedda in *I Pagliacci*

In the title role as Tchaikovsky's aloof aristocrat Eugene Onegin

As Don Giovanni in Mozart's and Lorenzo Da Ponte's realization of Don Juan

As Manfredo in Montemezzi's *L'Amore Dei Tre Re*, plotting the fate of his unfaithful wife and her lover

Scarpia basks in the pleasure he takes
from the "violent conquest" of women in *Tosca*

Photographs copyright Joan Marcus

As Scarpia with Shirley Verrett in a production of
Puccini's *Tosca* at Kennedy Center

As John Proctor in Robert Ward's *The Crucible*

~ *Allegro Con Brio*

~ My First AGMA Contract

Marguerite Ruffino had a finger in every pie. She ran a small opera company, in which she was the featured soprano. She had a big, loud, undisciplined voice and never quite learned her music. As a byproduct of her own shameless self-promotion, however, she created countless opportunities for young singers.

Her conductor was a pleasant guy named Tom Booth, a well-established accompanist and coach, and he was to become one of my first conductor friends. He appreciated my musical skills as much as my voice and requested me for baritone roles whenever possible. It was a rarity to have a real musician on the stage, and the guys in the pit appreciated it. Because I would accept any role and could jump in at a minute's notice, I became Marguerite's leading baritone. I learned Scarpia for her in only five days and performed the role without a mistake.

After an eternity of hacking around and mounting shows on minuscule budgets, Marguerite managed to get the funding to create a small professional company in Rhode Island. The premier production was *Carmen*, and she cast me as Escamillo, the toreador, in a much more established cast.

The new company, now named Artists Internationale, operated under the American Guild of Musical Artists, a union that governs opera, oratorio, symphonic singers, ballet dancers, and conductors. My first AGMA fee was one-hundred fifty dollars.

With this contract, and by virtue of hard work, determination, and being in the right place at the right time, I made a small crack in the seemingly impervious wall of the American opera scene.

I was now a union artist. I could see the future as clearly as the gray sludge covering New York City. I instinctively knew I would be doing this time and time again, on larger stages, in more and more distinguished company.

Whatever "it" was, I had it. There was no doubt now. All other interests, concerns, and desires would be sublimated to this goal. I had to sing better and be more prepared than my colleagues. My languages had to be perfect. Not one note could be out of place. I could not utter one hesitant phrase. I had to be stronger, tougher, and smarter than the competition to ascend the ladder of success. My sense of certainty for this outcome was indomitable—resolute.

Unfortunately, this increased sense of competition brought out my worst nature. As a child, I had never been the competitive sort, even in athletics. I often let others win at games just to be magnanimous. But now I cultivated a latent, inborn blood lust. I lunged fully into my Warrior Phase. My singing became the sole extension of my ego.

Most artists are neurotic in one way or another, but I crossed a line into an unwholesome place, as I began to define myself through my voice. Men typically do this with their careers, but I took the personification of The Voice to a new high. When I sang, women responded, men responded, doors opened. Those initially unimpressed with me, or even those who considered me an asshole, did a one-eighty the moment I sang. My identity became infused with my ability to create those deep, rich, mellifluous tones. The Voice and I were one. When people remarked at its beauty, they were remarking on my beauty, all physical imperfections erased. As long as I sang, I was highly desired. That thrill became an aphrodisiac of unparalleled intensity.

Guarding and nurturing this key to all realms became my sole focus and obsession. I sat at the piano for hours every day singing into a tape recorder, listening, re-recording. I'd find one perfect note then move a half-tone in one direction and match that tone to the last. Then I'd start the whole cycle over again.

There was a six-month period when I did nothing but work on one octave of my voice, from E natural above middle C to the E below. Listening, matching, singing, recording. I played recordings of the great baritones over and over. When I had their sound in my ear, I went back to the piano to sing, match, and record, again and again.

Except for gigs, lessons, and life's basic necessities, from waking until sleeping I did little else for almost two years. One day somewhere in the middle of 1974, I said, "Okay. I understand the art of making tone."

Subtle behaviors like this reinforced in me a sense of specialness, even separateness. But as a line from the *Desiderata* warns, "Do not compare yourself with others, or you may become vain and bitter. For always there will be greater and lesser persons than yourself."

~⤳ It's Only *Rigoletto*

One of the advantages of opera, being a kind of hermetically sealed art form, is that the components are easily interchangeable. Once you know a part, especially in a standard "stand and sing" opera, it's relatively easy to put a show together or slide somebody into an empty slot. And because opera is so expensive to mount, it's often the case that being instantaneous is an advantage. Mounting a performance on a low budget, little rehearsal, and a wing and a prayer is called "Instant Opera."

During my early years, I took full advantage of the many small opera companies in and around New York. My musical curiosity was insatiable, so if an opera struck my fancy, I sat at the piano and learned it. This was to prove very rewarding throughout my career, but especially in the beginning. Because of my musical skills, I could learn a role in Italian, French, or English and have it rehearsal-ready in about three weeks—even sooner, if the pressure was on.

The title role of *Rigoletto* is a mainstay of the baritone repertory. The opera is done all the time. And though the role is difficult because of its length, it fit me like a glove, sitting in the most opulent part of the baritone voice and providing plenty of opportunities to show off high notes. By age twenty-six, I had performed the role numerous times, mostly with piano or small orchestra. So when I received an offer from a local impresario to do it for the opening of a new theater in Connecticut, I was ready, willing, and able.

All the other members of the cast were people I had worked with before or knew through reputation. We had five days of rehearsal at the Ansonia, a once-luxurious residential hotel made famous by such residents as Enrico Caruso, Babe Ruth, Arturo Toscanini, and Igor Stravinsky. This was more than enough rehearsal for *Rigoletto*, and it seemed like another painless Instant Opera gig. The only wild card was the conductor. He was a young Spaniard from Juilliard, full of fire and undaunted by the task before him. And after all—it was only *Rigoletto*, an opera that practically plays itself.

On the first day of rehearsal, we started from the top. Immediately, my colleagues and I noticed the conductor was not flowing with us, musically speaking. While Verdi wrote straightforward, oom-pa-pa music for the orchestra, the opera includes several traditionally elongated stretches and held notes, not indicated in the printed music. To the singers' consternation, this young fellow often slashed through these lilting moments.

After a quick powwow with the cast, I was given the honor of approaching El Capitan to voice our concerns. I discovered he had done little preparation for the opera and had never even listened to a recording. In fact, he proclaimed, he was not very fond of opera—considering himself a symphonic conductor—and only took the job for the money and a notch on his resume. I took the bad news back to my colleagues, and we resolved to stop the rehearsal whenever necessary to "educate" him.

Another quirk about Instant Opera is that the small parts, or *comprimario* roles, are usually performed by people who have done those parts for decades. In New York, they are often members of the Italian community who do it solely for the love of the music. For this reason, and because of the "plug and play" nature of the standard operas, *comprimario* singers rarely attend rehearsals. For the three or four lines they sing, it's simply not necessary. Instead, just before the performance the director tells them where to enter, where to stand, and where to exit. This production was no different because, after all, it was only *Rigoletto*.

After five days of tense rehearsals, we did a grind-through at Juilliard. The orchestra members, though talented, had some very rocky moments—wrong notes, disastrous entrances, and general chaos. But everyone persisted, tempers were soothed, and the night of the performance finally arrived.

A large bus was procured to take the orchestra and cast back and forth to the theater. After a two-hour trip through some lovely countryside, we arrived at a picturesque little theater out in the middle of nowhere. The cast members found their dressing rooms, the orchestra headed to the Green Room, and preparations for the performance began.

I sat at my dressing room mirror, applying the last touches to my makeup as the dark strains of the overture began. *Oops!* I heard the same, incorrect chords I'd heard in the orchestra rehearsal piping through my monitor.

Did he forget to correct the parts? Could it be this guy can't hear it? No, couldn't be. It's just a fluke. Don't get anxious. It's only Rigoletto. What could go wrong?

What, indeed?

The first act went pretty smoothly. And the second. Then came the third, where Rigoletto storms into the Duke's castle, confronts his henchmen, and sings the magnificent aria "Cortigianni, Vil Razza! Dannata!" It is a moment for which opera lovers wait expectantly. The aria ends with a poignant duet between the baritone and a single cello.

Just before this breathtaking moment, a page, sung by a *comprimario*, rushes in with important news. Traditionally, the music accelerates slightly during the page's entrance. This *accelerando* is not marked in the musical score. Unrehearsed and, indeed, unheard until that very moment, our page ran onstage singing the faster tempo as she had in dozens of previous performances. In that instant, she jumped several measures ahead of the conductor's beat, pulling half of the orchestra with her. The conductor, whose head had been buried in the score until now, looked up with wild eyes. Unsure of what to do, he tried to change the beat, which only confused the orchestra further.

Kneeling at the edge of the proscenium, ready to launch into my aria, I watched in disbelief as the inconceivable happened. The orchestra skidded toward a train wreck as the conductor lost control. Random bleeps and toots emerged from the pit as, bit-by-bit, the music came to a grinding halt.

Silence in an opera is not a good thing.

Agonizing seconds passed. The audience began to murmur. Those of us onstage could do no more than wait. In the pin-drop hush, the conductor whispered something to the orchestra. The sound of rapidly turning pages filled the theater. The maestro suddenly brought down the stick, and music from the *next* scene poured from the pit. My aria, the sublime moment of Act III, had been cut.

Fortunately, hearing the chaos through her dressing room monitor, the soprano playing Gilda had rushed to the wings to witness the surreal fiasco, arriving just in time to hear her entrance cue. She ran onstage, somewhat breathless, to finish the scene. Neither of us moved during her aria or the duet that closes the act. We just sat there on the floor, staring at the idiot waving the baton until the curtain fell.

At intermission, I roared downstairs to the orchestra room with every intention of breaking bones. Maestro had locked himself in the bathroom and refused to come out until his antagonists disappeared. The impresario urged me to cool down until after the show, so I went back to my dressing room to stew.

We finished the show, collected our checks, and piled onto the bus for the ride home. The principal cellist came up to me as we boarded and said, "Hey, I'm sorry we didn't get to do our duet."

All I could do was offer a weak smile. "Yeah, well … it's only *Rigoletto*."

The conductor was never seen again. Supposedly, he got a ride back to Manhattan with friends, but it's difficult to believe he had any. A rumor circulated that he had annoyed the Wrong People. The production had been funded by one of New York's most notable "Families," if you know what I mean. It made sense. This was a beloved Italian opera, in an Italian community. I had seen lots of guys with dark suits and white ties seated in the audience. I never heard anything about the conductor again, nor the impresario, so … who knows? It would have been poetic justice. You don't butcher these people's music and get away with it.

I was philosophical about the experience. After all, I had escaped relatively unscathed. The worst that could happen in my career had happened, and everything that followed would be a cakewalk in comparison.

Oh, foolish boy. I had no clue, then, that this was just a preview of things to come.

❧ Managements

Of the hundreds of artists' managements listed in Musical America, the vast majority are located in New York, the hub of the nation's cultural wheel. Managements outside the Big Apple are small players in the grand scheme. While these organizations may provide a jumpstart for young artists who are reluctant to leave their region of the country, they rarely have the clout to nudge their clients into the uppermost reaches of the industry.

But, you may ask, isn't talent the only thing that counts? Well ... not exactly. Like all businesses, show business has its political side and its network of insidious alliances. These have created a stepping-stone hierarchy, like an obstacle course, which must be overcome before the contestant is allowed to reach for the Golden Ring—just like in politics.

Artists' managements, despicable as they may be, serve a crucial function. Managers act as sentinels for the music industry, as filters, constituting a first line of defense against no-talents. Like scientists in a Social Darwinist's dream, permitting only the strongest and smartest to spawn, managers are poised to weed out the unworthy. In order to sing for the plush jobs, you must know when and where the auditions are taking place. The companies, themselves, will not tell you. This information is only divulged to managers; therefore you must first pass their scrutiny.

Performing artists need a manager, unless they want to spend all their time spying on singers who have representation and attempting to crash *their* auditions. Some have tried this technique successfully, but I don't advise it, unless you thrive on confrontation or have *cojones* bigger than King Kong.

But the greatest reason managements exist is most performers are dreadful self-promoters. Selling is for salesmen—not artists. If and when you get an offer, it's always better to have somebody else negotiate the deal. Just as a real estate broker plays middleman—or woman—a manager deflects nasty issues about money that might create animosity between an artist and the company making the offer. They also negotiate conditions such as dressing-room preferences, rehearsal and performance dates, and all manner of perks. There are even tales of managers negotiating sexual favors. That's for another book.

I was fortunate to sing *Tosca* with Shirley Verrett a number of times. She always insisted on a clause in her contract that stipulated a two-day hiatus between performances. When an artist, even someone of Shirley's stature, makes personal demands like this, the star could be perceived as temperamental. But if a manager demands these perks, the impresario thinks the *manager* is the jerk.

I didn't sign with a management until I'd been in New York for almost eight years. It wasn't for want of trying; I just couldn't find an open slot with a reputable organization. Occasionally, managers I'd met socially recommended me for jobs, but I never felt that magic connection with them or them with me.

A manager-artist relationship is often more intimate than a marriage. Managers have to cope with the eccentricities of the artist as well as The Voice. A manager who does not have a deep understanding of singing and singers is rarely an effective conduit between artist and employer. Even after the artist's fee is negotiated and the contract signed, as the performance date approaches the manager sends out publicity packages and fields last-minute requests for interviews and public relations functions. All this, while keeping in mind the singer's rehearsal and performance schedule. A good manager nurtures singers as though they were temperamental thoroughbreds, acting as a barrier to the outside world so the artists can do what they've been born to do—perform beautifully.

Wise, scrupulous managers harbor only as many singers in their "stables" as they can efficiently provide for. Gross exceptions to this rule exist, of course—there are opportunists afoot in every business. Some small, independent managers make a living by discovering new talent and promising work, thus persuading them to pay large retainers, up front. As with anything that is pre-paid, this creates at least a temptation to slack off. Money in hand, some managers provide minimal publicity, schedule a few auditions, and consider their work complete. After all, nobody can guarantee you a job.

Legitimate managements work on a percentage basis. The standard fee is 10 percent of gross earnings, and, as most contracts are exclusive, very little work fails to pass through the manager's oversight. Some managers request their commissions up front, as soon as the contract is signed and sealed; others, upon completion of the contract.

You can look at this in two ways. On the one hand, the bulk of the manager's work is complete upon signing the contract, so they want their money. On the other, the contracted work is often years down the line (two to three years on average), so the artist may not have the funds available to pay a commission up front in a lean year.

The name of the game among managements is clout. When I was coming up, Columbia Artists Management, Inc. (CAMI) was the top power broker in the industry. Having gobbled up most of the big stars (as well as many promising upstarts, before they could fall into the clutches of rival managements), they bloated their roster with as many potential moneymakers as possible, as long as they were copasetic with the individual managers. Even though some smaller managements had a few illustrious stars to whom they catered, CAMI was the Mother of All Managements, and if you were a preferred horse in their stable, you always had a race to run.

Because CAMI had such a stranglehold on the industry, they had the power to offer opera companies package deals around a major star. This meant the company had to hire upcoming artists from the CAMI roster to fill out the cast. This was a symbiotic relationship for CAMI artists and the companies who were run by less-than-competent directors, as it allowed them simply to turn their casting decisions over to CAMI, and then sit back and take the credit if all went well. If it didn't, they'd play dumb and push the blame back on the management.

CAMI also ran a large concert series in order to flesh out the schedules of artists who had holes in their seasons, creating a financial cushion that allowed them to pay the bills while they were coasting between jobs. Not to mention the additional commissions for CAMI—pretty nifty.

Managements can also protect the fragile egos of their top clients by keeping rogue artists out of the loop.

A young conductor whose career was taking off at New York City Opera—without the benefit of management—was approached one day by an illustrious CAMI representative. Flattered by the attention and thinking he couldn't pass up the golden opportunity, the young man signed a long-term contract, after which CAMI just sat on him, essentially barring him from the plum jobs. These they funneled to their more renowned conductors.

Unable to fend for himself because he was under contract, he languished for years until he was able to break away. I'm not sure he ever recovered the ability to capitalize on his initial publicity. It's a tricky business. Land mines can be laid in the least likely places, even in seemingly friendly territory.

The three most powerful names in opera when I was a young singer were Matthew Epstein (a manager with CAMI), James Levine (music director of the Metropolitan Opera), and Robert Jacobson (editor of Opera News). They created a triumvirate that held opera hostage for decades. As a faction of the Gay Opera Mafia, the perception within the industry was that these three were in cahoots. They certainly moved in the same circles.

Epstein would promote a singer, who would conveniently get a series of rave reviews from Jacobson, and next thing you knew that singer was miraculously appearing at the Met under the baton of Levine.

This could have been an unrelated series of events, but considering that some very talented singers—who were far more deserving of a Met debut than Epstein's Wonder-of-the-Day—were languishing in relative obscurity, it only served to create more cynicism.

Over those years, Epstein managed to entice many flowering artists into the CAMI stable. And an impressive stable it was. While those of us on the outside found the cliquish atmosphere surrounding this crowd distasteful—no doubt because we were not invited to the party—in all fairness, music is a very subjective game, and tastes follow the times. And *they* were setting the trends. If I'd had their power, I probably would have done the same thing.

～ Louise

Parties at Aldo's apartment on West 72nd street were Events, with a capital "E." The lavish fests at the home of the young Felix Mendelssohn must have been very similar. Artists from every discipline socialized and performed. Aldo's living room/studio housed two grand pianos, and it was not uncommon to hear everything from concertos to musical theater and from opera to actors' monologues. It was spectacular.

I met Louise Williams at one such party. She was a friend of a friend and had come by chance. Louise had been involved with the Metropolitan Auditions for many years. These auditions were a big deal in the industry, culminating in a Final Audition every year on the stage of the Met. Louise had recently decided to go off on her own as an artists' manager. To make a long story short, we met at Aldo's party. I sang, and within a few days I signed an exclusive contract.

During our several years together, Louise saw me through a divorce, numerous love affairs, huge emotional ups and downs, and financial troubles. Because of her determination and stead-fast belief in my talent, I traveled from anonymity to notoriety through countless debuts and successes. She derived the satisfaction of escorting me to the realm of established artist.

When we both were living in Los Angeles in the mid-1980s, Louise was diagnosed with breast cancer. Unbeknownst to me, she had beaten it once before. She suspected it had returned but was waiting for her Medicare benefits to kick in before she went for another diagnosis. As it turned out, she waited too long. The tumor had metastasized into her rib cage. The surgeon removed a large chunk of breastbone over her heart, leaving a gaping hole. I took her home after the surgery and carried her up the stairs to her apartment. She weighed almost nothing. She tried to exist there on her own for a few days before we had to transfer her to a cancer hospital in downtown Los Angeles.

I made the hellish drive through L.A. traffic to see her every day for the next few weeks, until I had to go to Detroit to sing Tonio in *Pagliacci*. The day I left was the last time I saw her. Penny, my longtime companion, stayed with her up to the moment they pulled the plug. Neither my life nor my career was ever the same.

For a short time, I worked with another manager I'd met many years before in San Francisco, but we just weren't in sync. I negotiated with a few others, but nothing seemed to click. Finally, I experimented with self-management for awhile, before the un-raveling began.

I've often felt relieved that Louise wasn't there for the end of my career. She would never have stopped crying.

San Francisco

In autumn 1974, I was offered a contract from Western Opera Theater, the touring subsidiary of San Francisco Opera. I wasn't thrilled about maintaining two apartments, but the money was decent and the job paid per diem while on tour. It would be a stretch, but it was doable. The irresistible temptation was the repertory: Figaro in *The Barber of Seville*, Germont in *La Traviata*, the Villains in *The Tales of Hoffman*, and a small part in Bernstein's *Trouble in Tahiti*.

My wife and I decided I would go to San Francisco, she would stay in Manhattan, and we'd arrange to get together whenever we could. It wasn't an ideal arrangement, but we agreed it was a prime opportunity, and we resolved to make the best of it.

I arrived in the Gay Bay on a rainy day in September. I found an apartment on Knob Hill, halfway between Chinatown and the Polk Street restaurants.

Rehearsals took place in an old, poorly heated building behind the opera house. I arrived the first day to find myself in a group of twelve singers, three piano/conductors, a couple of intermittent stage directors, a costume coordinator, and miscellaneous crew members. They were to be my family away from home for the next eight months.

When one of the tenors cancelled the tour at the last minute, I recommended my friend Keith Baker. The managers hired him, and he flew out immediately. We had a blast and made some wonderful friendships.

Except for the typical quarrels and power struggles that occur within any family, the tour was an artistic and anthropological success. We learned how to travel for hours on a bus without killing each other and how to sing on command—both good skills. In six months we toured most of Arizona, California, Oregon, Washington, Idaho, and Utah, enjoying all of it, from the free samples at Olympia Brewery in the Pacific Northwest to the abandoned turquoise mines of Bisbee, Arizona.

At the end of the tour, we had a brief respite in San Francisco before starting a series of performances around the city. During this break I heard about an award established by Bruce Yarnell's widow, Kathy, in his memory. I auditioned and became the first recipient of the Bruce Yarnell Award for Young Baritones. I sang well, but the fact that I was the only competitor to have worked with Bruce in summer stock probably didn't hurt my chances, either.

This bit of good publicity and my successes during a season of touring created a blip on the radar screen, and the powers that presided over San Francisco Opera took notice. Kurt Herbert Adler, perhaps the most powerful and caustic member of the old Austrian Jewish Mafia, still reigned supreme here. Through his considerable staff of henchmen, he offered me a few secondary roles in the upcoming season, as well as the matinee performances of *L'Elisir D'Amore* and the title role in *Don Giovanni*. My original nine-month stay had been extended to a year and a half.

It was a spectacular experience, full of parties, celebrations, and events—San Francisco-style. I was even featured at one of these soirées, singing the seduction duet from *Don Giovanni* with a countertenor to a giddy audience of San Francisco Queens. They just love that kind of camp.

That season was my first encounter with a multitude of international artists, directors, and conductors. I worked with a long list of luminaries, and I drew a few conclusions from those experiences that were reinforced over the years.

First, I don't like British conductors. They're often smarmy, asinine, and pompous—usually without the talent to back it up.

German stage directors make German conductors look like amateurs when it comes to obsessive-compulsive disorder. One guy named Rennert spent days of rehearsal moving each person on the stage three inches at a time, demanding that we memorize our exact locations. Then he changed everything in the next rehearsal. It was maddening. Directors are generally the repressed, frustrated wannabe performers of the industry, and most of them should be locked in institutions.

The silver lining to these engagements in the big house was my opportunity to work with each of The Three Tenors, long before they were dubbed by that name.

In addition to being cast in small roles in *Il Coranazione di Popea* and *Andrea Chénier*, and the baritone lead in *L'Elisir d'Amore*, I was assigned to cover Count Di Luna in *Il Trovatore* and was therefore obligated to attend rehearsals. But this was a bonus, considering *Trovatore*'s stellar cast: Australian soprano Joan Sutherland, Italian tenor Luciano Pavarotti, Russian mezzo Elena Obraztsova, and Swedish baritone Invar Wixell.

Sutherland, one of the great divas of the twentieth century, was making her first foray into this repertory, yet she always appeared mellow and low-key. She had been at the top of the game so long that the process of singing and rehearsing seemed almost like an afterthought. Her husband and mentor, Richard Bonynge, conducted.

Pavarotti was also said to be doing Manrico for the first time, although I found this difficult to believe. His career had received a huge bump after Sutherland recommended him for a number of productions in the late sixties. By 1975 he was an enormous star with his own following. He was an extreme extrovert, joking constantly and splashing himself with cologne. I always assumed this was to mask his profuse sweating. Many critics thought Manrico was too big for him at this stage in his career, but he made fools of those critics.

Despite the tremendous singing of Sutherland and Pavarotti, for my money, Elena Obraztsova was the highlight of the cast. I had never heard Azucena sung with such force and passion. I'm not sure whether she was quiet or spoke little English, but she stayed to herself and rarely spoke during rehearsals.

Ingvar Wixell was a jolly, good-natured fellow. His voice reminded me of Dietrich Fischer-Dieskau on steroids. He employed that airy, Germanic tone and sang "open" all the way through the upper voice, with a top-out at around G-flat. It was sometimes painful to listen to, but it was loud, which is never a bad thing in opera.

I was also double-cast with Wixell as Belcore in *L'Elisir*. He did the evening performances, and I sang the matinees. The tenor in his cast was a young Jose Carreras, only two years my senior, whose career was on a rocket sled. After his operatic debut in 1970, he had catapulted from NYCO to the Met in only four short years. While he was a bit short on stagecraft, even then it was apparent he had a voice of extraordinary beauty that would take him far.

The director, Lotfi Mansouri—later to become the fourth general director of San Francisco Opera—browbeat Carreras in rehearsal, criticizing him for almost every move and gesture. Despite the fledgling status of his career, I was surprised Jose took it. Mansouri was a polished and talented director, yet I rarely felt comfortable working with him. A master of physical characterization, he usually had rigid, preconceived ideas about how each character should look and move that were not necessarily congruent with the artist cast in the part.

I did my first Jack Rance in *La Fanciulla del West* under Lotfi's direction a year later. He was adamant that Jack was a portly man of substantial weight and worked with me on developing a broad, heavy gait. There's nothing in the score to indicate Rance's stature or physical attributes, yet Mansouri was insistent that I try to adopt *his* physicalization. He even considered padding me for the part. Meanwhile, here I was, almost six feet tall, a-hundred-and-forty pounds, and rapier thin. A more creative director uses the physical traits and skill sets of his actors to create homogenized characterizations. But this was not Lotfi's way, and though we had a congenial working relationship over a number of productions, we never really hit it off.

The best thing about this season in San Francisco was getting to know Placido Domingo. He was singing the title role in *Andrea Chénier* with a powerful cast, including baritone Cornel MacNeil, late in his career. The next year I would get to know "Big Mac" a lot better when we were double-cast as Jack Rance. He was once one of the greatest baritones ever to grace the operatic stage, but in person I found him generally surly, ill-natured, and not easy to interact with.

Placido was another story. He was, and remains, one of the finest human beings in the business. Affable, good natured, and a superlative artist—both musically and dramatically—he was always available to his colleagues, regardless of their stature or prominence.

This was an early *Chénier* for Domingo, even though he celebrated his 1100th performance during this run—an astonishing accomplishment, when you compare it with some famous singers like Maria Callas who had many fewer performances in their entire careers. As of this writing, Placido has sung more than 3500 performances.

I vividly remember the opening night of *Chénier*. As I passed the open door to Placido's dressing room on my way to the stage, he sat socializing with other cast members. On a table near the door, a bottle of white wine chilled in a bucket of ice. In his hand was a nearly empty glass. Astonished, I asked him how he could drink and sing. Laughing, he replied, "I need it to get through 'The Improviso.'"

As I'll discuss later, I've known three people who emitted unmistakable auras. That night, Placido displayed the first I'd ever seen. It was during his first act aria "Un di, all azzurro spazio," also called "The Improviso." It's the first highly dramatic moment in the opera and a terrifying aria for many tenors. Maybe it was the wine or maybe just his stupendous talent, but Placido shimmered with this bluish-purple aura as he sang and received one of the most spectacular ovations I've ever heard in person.

We were to work together two more times, both in *La Fanciulla del West*, and I fondly remember him coming backstage to congratulate me when I debuted the production at NYCO some years later. I found more to admire in this man every time I met him. I especially admired his trait of never speaking ill of another colleague, kind of his own version of Ronald Reagan's Eleventh Commandment. It's common in this business to sit around like a bunch of old biddies, gossiping about your colleagues' personal lives or dissecting their technique. There's usually an element of enmity and pettiness in these discussions, but Placido would have none of it. If a conversation turned in that direction, he would immediately change the subject. What a *mensch*!

The only truly dark spot in my year in San Francisco was an Opera in the Parks production of *Don Giovanni*.

Bob Darling—whom we unaffectionately called "Darling Bob Darling" when he was out of earshot—was one of the most arrogant, talentless pricks I've ever met. I have no problem saying that, because I know he feels exactly the same way about me. This guy was a set designer who had made the transition to stage direction through some misguided advice. This is not necessarily a logical or lateral progression. Designing sets and understanding how to move actors around on them creatively are different skills altogether.

This was a modern-dress production, in which Don Juan was a rock star and Leporello his chauffeur. Darling Bob had previously mounted this production somewhere in Buttfuck, USA, and I suppose his inexpensive sets were SFO's motivation for bringing him aboard.

I was suspicious about this guy after the first rehearsal, when we did nothing more than improvise one scene for two hours. Improvisation has it place in a theatrical setting, but the opening scene to Giovanni is not it. When a director does something like this, before discussing characterization and doing some basic blocking, it's usually a sign he isn't prepared.

As rehearsals progressed, I became more and more uneasy. When Darling finally started making choices, he had us doing things that were quirky, incongruous, and downright absurd.

The final straw came as we started blocking the last scene, during which the statue of the Commendatore comes to life and demands that Giovanni repent for his crimes. Giovanni refuses, and the gates of Hell open as demons crawl out of the earth and drag him to eternal damnation. Great stuff!

There we were, ready to stage this powerful scene, the culmination of two hours of singing, with boiling music in D-minor swelling toward the grand finale. Darling Bob Darling says, "Now at this point, you tear off your robe, pick up the candelabras, and put the candles out on your bare chest, punishing yourself for your crimes. Then I want you to writhe on the empty stage until the music ends."

Well, maybe Sir Lawrence Olivier could have pulled this off, but I couldn't even imagine how to make it work. The scene from *The Goodbye Girl* where the director tells Richard Dreyfus to play a lisping, mincing, Richard III sprang to mind. In my nicest, are-you-fucking-kidding-me voice, I said, "What!? You've got to be out of your mind!"

"No, I'm not. The last guy who I directed did it, and it works. You're going to do it, too."

"Is that so?" said I, on the edge of losing control.

How about I put my fist through your face first?

Sensing a fight was about to break out, the bass who was singing Leporello stepped between us, took me aside, and persuaded me to at least try it. I did. It was dreadful, but I agreed to think about it and see if I could find some motivation for this ludicrous staging.

I arrived at the next rehearsal with a list of other ideas and experimented with them while the rehearsal pianist played the music. Darling Bob Darling sat watching with his arms crossed. When he finally couldn't take it anymore, he rushed to the prop table, grabbed the candelabras, and ran to the stage.

"Here, use the candles! It's ridiculous without them!" he screamed, pushing them toward me.

"I've got news for you, pal—it's ridiculous *with* them!" I hollered, then pitched the candelabras across the stage and stomped out.

That was our last direct communication. We ignored each other's presence for the rest of the rehearsal period. This couldn't have been very comfortable for the other cast members, but they grinned and bore it. They, too, were unhappy with much of the staging, but nobody else had the balls to tell this clown what an idiot he was.

A director's main function is to act as a traffic cop by setting entrances and exits and moving people around so they aren't bumping into one another. As the dress rehearsal arrived, most of us still had no idea when and where our entrances were. We had spent so much time toying with inane little stage bits that we never actually finished blocking the opera. Two hours had been set aside for the dress rehearsal, and we were nowhere near the end. At the two-hour mark, in the middle of the last act, I looked at my watch and announced rehearsal was over. I removed my costume and went home as the others continued to rehearse.

Next day I was called in to see Adler's associate, a guy who later went on to work at the National Endowment for the Arts. He asked me what the problem was.

I said, "Look, this guy is moron and you don't have to stand out there making a fool of yourself in front of all those people!

I'm not doing the candle bit. Let him be creative and come up with something else, or replace me!"

He vowed that he would talk with Darling and voiced a hope that I would cooperate in the meantime.

They didn't replace me, and the performances were a sham. It was the first time in my career where I simply clocked in, did my thing, packed up my makeup, and went home.

I was never asked back to San Francisco Opera, and these events nourished a cynicism about the business that would stay with me for a long time.

⤳ Houston

After San Francisco, I spent four months with Houston Grand Opera, where I was contracted to sing four roles in succession: Iago in *Otello*, Titus Thumb in the World Premier of *Bilby's Doll*, the title role in *Don Giovanni*, and Jack Rance in *La Fanciulla del West*.

I made a good friend here who was also contracted to sing throughout the season. Jacque Trussel—known simply as Jack in those days—was an eccentric, to say the least, and susceptible to fads. He traveled with an armada of equipment for his health regime, including a collapsible trampoline and trunks full of special foods. He perfected the art of living comfortably on the road. For him, this meant transporting most of his life with him, tortoise-style.

Bald as a billiard ball yet charming and charismatic, Jack was very popular with the ladies. He always had something going on with somebody interesting. He was capable of being both social and aloof at the same time. I envied his ability to switch between those two diametrically opposed interactions as easily as one would flick on a light switch.

Jack knew every odd, hole-in-the-wall health-food place in the country. During one of our visits to the land of soy sprouts and mung beans, he hooked many of his colleagues, including me, on biorhythms. This theory originated in the nineteenth century with Wilhelm Fliess, a Berlin physician, numerologist, and good friend and patient of Sigmund Freud.

Depending on whom you ask, biorhythm is considered either a protoscience or pseudoscience. Based on one's birth date, it calculates certain predetermined cycles, said to forecast physiological, emotional, and intellectual processes, and predicts how these are likely to affect your interactions with the world around you.

Jack, who could have been a great salesman, talked a number of us into purchasing plastic calculators that showed how the three rhythms flowed and coincided. When the cycles were at their peak, it was time to be brave, assertive, make the world your oyster. When the cycles were low, it was best to withdraw and become reflective.

Singers will do almost anything to predict how they're going to feel on any given day, especially performance days. They'll grasp at the finest straw if they think it will give them an edge. So naturally, we all started compulsively tracking our biorhythms.

I have to say that sometimes I would be in a funk, unable to concentrate or relate to others and, by God, I'd check the calculator and find myself low in all three rhythms. There were nights when I sang like a god and I'd check my biorhythm. Wow, a triple high! All three rhythms were peaking at the same time! Maybe there was something to this stuff.

Whether it worked or not, it made me feel I was somehow in control of my life, that maybe everything wasn't random chaos in an existential universe that conspired to suck me into a black hole. I continued to religiously follow my biorhythms.

Then one day, I phoned Jack to see if he wanted to go out to lunch. He whispered in a conspiratorial tone that he dared not leave his apartment—he had a triple critical and would call me when it was safe to come out.

Click.

I sauntered over to my nightstand, snatched up the little plastic biorhythm calculator, and threw it in the trash. Sometime later, at the suggestion of a numerologist, Jack changed his name to "Jacque." His career immediately took off, ultimately landing him at the Met.

Back to Houston.

Like a few other companies, Houston double-cast the shows. Established stars would perform the operas in the original language, and youthful upstarts like me would sing in English and stand by for the Big Guns. It was good for everybody concerned.

Houston had a very young general director named David Gockley. At first, I took a strong liking to him. But ultimately he proved to be a ball-less wonder who, in my opinion, buckled to a powerful artists' management while hiding in his office, unavailable for comment.

Otello went well, except the tenor in the Italian cast became ill. The tenor in my cast replaced him, accomplishing a tour-de-force that I doubt has been equaled to this day: He sang Otello, a murderously difficult part, three times in less than thirty-six hours. Unheard of, but that's why shows are double cast. It's a back-up system worth its weight in gold.

Sherrill Milnes and I were double-cast as Iago in this production. Remember him? The Tonio in the first opera I ever saw? Milnes proved to be a genuinely nice guy, if a bit pompous. But, hey, he earned it. He was large in stature and possessed a clear voice with a wonderful high range. Unlike some of his predecessors, his languages and musicianship were impeccable. He was the noble ruler of the Baritone Realm for many years.

When we were out having drinks one night, Sherrill gave me one of the best singer's quotes I ever heard. We were discussing the trials of singing while ill, and he said, "When I get in trouble I stick it in the nose and push!"

By "it" he meant the tone. If you've ever heard Sherrill sing, you would appreciate the candidness of that statement.

Also, he was uncommonly generous. When my dresser disappeared during my dress rehearsal, Sherrill materialized out of nowhere to help me into my costume. Afterward, he came backstage with notes and some very good suggestions. I was deeply moved to get such input from the leading baritone of the decade and will always remember him with appreciation.

The second opera was the world premiere of *Bilby's Doll,* an opera by Carlyle Floyd, who also composed *Of Mice and Men.* This was a bitch to learn, because the only available score was a nearly illegible, handwritten manuscript, which had us constantly guessing what pitches and rhythms were intended. Not until Floyd arrived in Houston a short time before opening did we discover what he'd really written. But relearning something you've learned wrong is more difficult than learning it right to begin with, so many things stayed wrong in the performance. Fortunately, a lot of the score was atonal and dissonant, so aside from a few fingernails-on-a-blackboard moments, the errors were unnoticeable. Sometimes, they actually sounded better.

This opera, in English, was also double-cast. The first cast featured better-known singers. My counterpart was baritone Alan Titus, whose fame came through some well-publicized productions at NYCO and elsewhere. He had a serviceable if undistinguished voice, but he had a nice look and a good stage presence. Most important, he was on Matthew Epstein's roster at CAMI.

Both casts intermingled quite a bit during rehearsal, and as the run neared its end, Alan took me aside and said, "I'd stay close to the opera house on closing night, if I were you."

What?

He told me he'd been offered another gig for the evening of

his last performance, and because the other fee was much larger, he was thinking of ditching Houston. I'd heard of this sort of thing before, but I'd never seen it in action. He went on to elaborate.

"If I call in sick, they'll be in a bind. Have your manager ask for my fee, which I'm sure is much more than you're getting, and I'll split it with you."

I was not only dumbfounded, but because of his proposal, I faced a difficult ethical dilemma. I had no idea what to do. Alan must have seen the doubt in my eyes and thought better of his offer. He quickly made light of his suggestion and brushed it off as a joke.

Nonetheless, the cat was out of the bag, and I waited on pins and needles until the day arrived. By golly if didn't I get a call from the opera house that afternoon with the news that Mr. Titus was out of town and indisposed. Would I please come and sing the role tonight? *Well, well, well.*

I didn't have a manager at the time, so I decided to play the fee issue by ear. I arrived in my dressing room to find David Gockley waiting. He offered me a fee I knew was far lower than what he was paying Alan, but to avoid conflict I accepted.

Perhaps he saw something in my face—it's hard to know—but quite surprisingly, he said to me, "I have a feeling Alan isn't really sick."

Dead silence.

I felt like an informer who was being interrogated for information about some heinous crime. I was on the grill, and a number of ambiguous thoughts ran through my mind. My motives became perverse and noble all at once.

One Pollyanna voice said: *Alan is a colleague, one of us. You shouldn't betray him. But, hey, when you sign a contract, you make a commitment and ignore other offers.*

A competitive voice said: *David, I'm four times the baritone that clown is, and you're gonna offer me a quarter of what he's getting? I should get a sudden case of laryngitis, too, and tell you to go fuck yourself!*

Still another voice said: *Hey, David, I like you. Don't you know Columbia Artists has you by the short ones? You need to get some balls, be a fucking man, and kick Matthew Epstein and his cronies the hell out of Houston!*

After what seemed like an eternity of grappling with these arguing factions, I decided I should do the right thing. Gockley would be grateful to know how things really went down, I reasoned. He'd appreciate my honesty and realize he needed people like me around. I'd rat out my colleague, CAMI would be put in its place, and I'd be offered some plum roles in Houston as my reward.

Huge miscalculation!

I spilled the beans. Alan denied any such conversation ever took place and even got a note from his doctor to prove it.

Can you fucking believe that?

CAMI was up in arms. I became persona non grata for the rest of the Houston season and moved into the Top Ten on Matthew Epstein's hit list.

I did my work, and despite all the underlying darkness, I thoroughly enjoyed a very good production of Giovanni, where I played the debonair swashbuckler to the hilt. I got to swing across the stage from a chandelier and die in flames and perdition instead of extinguishing candles on my chest.

Then I explored the darkness of Jack Rance in *Fanciulla*, which was to become one of my favorite operas.

So, I left Houston, never to be invited back, despite my later successes. I'd been ostracized from two major houses in a row: Houston and San Francisco. Pretty good batting average. If I kept this up, I could start looking for a sheep ranch in Montana and forget this silly business altogether.

Maybe I should have checked my biorhythm.

❧ *Cadenza*

❧ Auditions: Being Your Own Judge

It's been postulated that a woman decides whether or not she's going to have sex with a man within ten minutes of their first meeting. No matter how charming, polite, and thoughtful he may be, his prospects for the night are determined with those initial impressions. Whoever came up with this aphorism was pretty astute, and I'd agree—except I think most women decide within the first ten *seconds*.

Auditions are a lot like a first date. You enter a room with your best smile. Introductions are made as you're scanned, appraised, and "typed." If you're the type they're looking for, you have about sixteen bars of music or a few lines of dialogue to woo them. If they've already typed you out in their minds, your performance is irrelevant—you can flatter like Don Juan, sing like Pavarotti, or intone like Olivier, but it won't make the slightest difference. You're going home alone to a cold shower.

Sometimes in theater auditions, they're considerate enough to have the hopefuls line up, ten at a time. Then they pick two or three they'd like to hear and say to the others, "Thank you very much. Please exit by the side door." This mercifully saves you the humiliation of putting on a mini-performance for somebody who couldn't care less. It's a meat market, and nobody pretends it's anything else.

Opera auditions work a little differently. Your vocal type is generally more important than your look. You're covered by heavy makeup and draped in a huge costume, so as long as you don't look like the Elephant Man (which, come to think of it, might actually be an advantage in some operas) it's the vocal performance that counts.

I learned early on that "short and sweet" is the rule of thumb for an audition. I always started with something splashy and flamboyant, made my impression, and got the hell out. Then I tried to forget about the experience altogether. I would not allow my mind to linger on the possible outcome of my audition, because it made me feel anxious, frustrated, and helpless. Instead, I made a game out of it. My job became learning how to give great audition and make that an end in itself.

Even under ideal circumstances, an audition is a nerve-wracking ordeal, and opera auditions are the best of the bunch. Your mind must be so focused on what you're doing it's nearly impossible to be objective about your performance.

The tendency after an audition is to go home and sit and wait for the phone to ring. When it doesn't, you go through an unproductive cycle of self-flagellation and doubt. Soon you begin to question your talent, undermining the entire purpose of your efforts.

I was trapped in this noxious thinking, once upon a time, but I found a way around it. I bought a high-quality, portable tape recorder and began taping my lessons, practice sessions, rehearsals, performances and—most important—my auditions. As I entered the room I'd leave my briefcase near the door, punch "Record," take the music to the pianist, and sing. Afterward, I would go home and listen. It was amazing how different I sounded on the tape than I did in my shaky memory of the audition. Like a mirror, the tape never lied.

This single act was more responsible than anything in providing me with a balanced view of my development. Moreover, it made it possible for me to persist, even when I was not offered the job. It provided a means of evaluating my singing completely separate from any feedback or lack thereof. My only task became to sing in a way that I, and I alone, would find acceptable. I was convinced the parameters of excellence to which I was striving had universal appeal. So, like an author, I just needed to find my audience.

I also used the recordings to enhance my ear and better translate what the voice in my head actually sounded like. This provided a marvelous advantage over singers of the past. Before the advent of recording devices, singers had to depend on coaches for that kind of feedback, and those impressions were subjective. You'll relate to what I mean if you think of the first time you heard your speaking voice on tape and thought, "That doesn't sound like me at all!" Singing sounds are even more surreal on playback.

After returning from San Francisco, I had the opportunity to sing for a second Rockefeller grant in New York. The Rockefeller Foundation had given me a study grant two years before, and I was hoping to get another. Grants were usually five thousand dollars—a lot of money in those days.

My first audition had not been to my liking but, miraculously, I won the grant. This second time around I was a more seasoned artist, and my voice had grown in size and dimension. As far as I was concerned, the audition was going to be a mere formality. Nonetheless, I chose tough pieces: the Prologue to *Pagliacci* and a little-known aria from Howard Hansen's *Merry Mount*—a tour-de-force for baritone. I strode onto the stage and, to put it quite modestly, sang like a god. Everything worked: high, low, middle, forte, piano—*tutto*! After the audition, I listened to the tape and felt assured it was a slam dunk.

A few weeks later I was invited to meet with the woman who administered the grants. I had diligently practiced my "gracious act," sprinkling it with dashes of gratitude about the Foundation's generosity. I even speculated that I might get more than I'd asked for.

As I entered her office, she invited me to sit. In her nicest voice, she asked how I thought I'd sung in the audition. Without hesitation, I said I thought I'd done extremely well. So, you can imagine my surprise when, with a face that looked like she'd bitten into a lemon, she said, "We've decided not to award you a grant this year." I looked at her in disbelief and did nothing to hide my shock. She handed me a breakdown of the jurors' comments. While they were not uncomplimentary, they weren't raves either. She asked, "What do you think?"

Perhaps I should have shown a bit more diplomacy, but instead I said, "It's bullshit! I taped this audition. I've listened to it countless times, and I'm telling you, it was great."

Not at all ready for this response, she gasped, "You taped the audition?"

"Yes, I tape all my auditions for circumstances just like this. If I sing well and receive critiques like these, I can be assured the judges were idiots. Not me."

Hardly knowing how to respond, she stammered something about how different panels of judges come up with completely different conclusions, and I was welcome to audition again, and so on. I stood quickly, told her I'd think about it, and left.

A few months later, I was offered a contract at New York City Opera. I made a copy of the offer and sent it to the woman at Rockefeller along with a note to the effect that perhaps the professionals of the music industry were better able to recognize talent than the Foundation's jurors. Oh, and by the way, thanks, but I'll pass on another audition.

I must say it gave me enormous glee to stand up for myself like that. But without the reassurance of that tape recording, I'm not sure I would have been able to do it.

❧ NYCO Encore

During my time in Houston, my manager had been planning an audition for New York City Opera. It wasn't difficult to get an audition at NYCO, but arranging one's schedule to accommodate available slots could be tricky. Because the New York State Theater was built for theater and ballet, it had notoriously poor acoustics. Nonetheless, this hall was the main proving ground for young American singers. A contract here was a necessity for those starting a career here in the States.

I had arranged an audition before leaving the extra chorus at NYCO to head out into the world as a soloist. Although Aldo never liked to play auditions, I persuaded him this was too important to leave in the hands of another pianist. He agreed. My voice was still growing and, though I sang well, Aldo's brilliant pianistic performance on the difficult piece eclipsed my own. Some of my colleagues from the chorus sneaked into the house and listened. They gave me some nice feedback, but the consensus was nobody would ever emerge from the chorus to become a soloist—and neither would I. I reminded them that Leonard Warren was once in the chorus at Radio City Musical Hall and went on to become the most heralded baritone of his era.

Five years had passed, my voice had blossomed, and I had a suitcase full of experience to bring to the table. After my Houston debacle, I made time to study and recuperate. I was in fine form. Louise scheduled an audition, and Aldo agreed to play for me once again.

Aldo and I lived a block away from each other, so we met at the corner of 72nd and Broadway and walked the ten blocks to Lincoln Center. The New York State Theater shares a plaza with the Met and Avery Fisher Hall, home of the New York Philharmonic.

As we walked past the fountain in the center of the plaza, we stood and looked at the three structures. They represented the pinnacle of classical music in New York. I took a deep breath.

Aldo said, in his familiar tone, "How do you feel?"

"As good as I'm ever going to feel."

"You're ready. Let's do it."

Then he gave me a fatherly pat on the back, and we set off for the stage door.

We went down the steps into the entrance, signed in, and waited our turn. After about ten minutes, my name was called. I strode onto the familiar stage to sing for Julius Rudel, John White, Felix Popper, and Thomas Martin. I knew Popper and Martin from an opera workshop I had taken at the Leiderkranz Foundation a number of years before. John White was administrative director and Rudel the artistic director and principal conductor. He was the one who needed convincing.

Once again, Aldo provided magnificent support as I sang the Prologue to Pagliacci. It was a wonderful feeling to sing alone on that stage. I could feel my voice resonate in the house, and I had a genuinely good time. When I was finished, somebody out in the house said, "Thank you," and that was that. I acknowledged the silhouettes in the darkness; we retraced our steps and headed uptown. Aldo returned to his studio, and I went home to listen to the tape of the audition. I was happy with what I heard but tried my best to keep my enthusiasm in perspective. It was said that Beverly Sills auditioned three times for City Opera before being offered a contract.

That evening the phone rang. It was Louise.

"Congratulations," she said. "You're going to make your New York City Opera debut as Alfio in *Cavalleria Rusticana*. John White said he hopes to have you at NYCO for a long time."

I hyperventilated. While I had envisioned this clearly, I still couldn't believe my ears. Not only had I made the impossible leap from chorus to leading baritone, but I had done it in one audition. The first one didn't really count, as far as I was concerned.

In the fall of 1977, at age twenty-nine, I stepped onto the stage of the New York State Theater as a leading NYCO baritone. I had found a home in a repertory company that provided a safe haven from the unpredictable world on the outside. It was the beginning of a ten-year relationship where I would eventually sing a dozen roles.

But in the midst of my joy, Robert Burns' words echoed in a far corner of my mind:

> But Mousie, thou art no thy lane,
> In proving foresight may be vain:
> The best laid schemes o' mice an' men
> Gang aft agley,
> An' lea'e us nought but grief an' pain,
> For promis'd joy!

✒ Menotti and Barber

During my life, I've encountered only three people who emitted an energy—a presence so strong I actually thought I could see an aura around them. The first and greatest was Muhammad Ali, during an exhibition bout in Miami. The second was onstage with Placido Domingo during the first act of *Andrea Chénier*. And the third was the Italian-American composer Gian Carlo Menotti.

Menotti was, without question, one of the most fascinating people I've ever known. As one of the few successful contemporary opera composers, he held a very special place in the opera world. His music is intense and brooding, filled with marvelous dissonances and abrupt key changes that really jar you. It's like Puccini on acid. In fact, in a reflective moment one day, he told me, quite matter-of-factly, he believed he was Puccini reincarnated. But with Gian Carlo, you never knew if he was saying something he meant or trying to shock you.

Our first meeting came out of the blue. I had just debuted at NYCO, and the hubbub had started about this slim, handsome, young baritone on the opera scene. Well, that kind of talk always attracted Menotti's attention, and his people arranged for an audition through my manager. He was preparing a revival of one of his lesser-known operas in Spoleto, Italy, and after seeing my publicity photo, he decided he wanted to hear me for the part.

An audition was scheduled at Samuel Barber's apartment on upper Fifth Avenue. Menotti and Barber had been linked for many years. Barber, of course, was another successful American composer, known for his opera *Vanessa* and the haunting "Adagio for Strings" that provides the musical backdrop for the movie *Platoon*.

A strikingly handsome young man met me at the door. As I entered, I saw he was one of a rather large retinue of young men lined up along the hallway, all greeting me with that certain smile I recognized from my summer-stock days. I was escorted down a long hallway to a studio at the far end. An L-shaped sofa occupied one corner and a grand piano the opposite corner. On the sofa, side by side, sat Menotti and Barber.

I don't remember any introductions or either of them speaking to me directly, but somehow I knew it was time to sing. I started with the Prologue to *Pagliacci*. They carried on a hushed conversation the entire time. In such an intimate space, their murmuring was more than a bit distracting, but I forged ahead. After singing the Prologue, Menotti asked if I had anything lower, so I pulled out "Nulla. Silenzio" from *Il Tabarro*. They really seemed to like this choice, but it was difficult to know.

When I finished, Barber thanked me, and I was escorted once again past the chorus line of lingering lackeys to the elevator. I had no idea what to make of the experience or what to expect. Their reactions were noncommittal. But I had survived yet another audition, so I rewarded myself with a stroll through Central Park.

As I walked through my front door, the phone rang. It was Louise, telling me that a contract was already in the mail. This served as another example of how impossible it was to second-guess these situations. Sometimes, auditioners would smile and nod, and then you'd never hear from them. Other times they'd sit with a dour expression, barely acknowledging your existence, and ten minutes later they'd promise you the world.

I had always assumed Menotti and Barber had tendered the contract because they'd been blown away by my singing. Years later at dinner with Menotti, I asked him why he had decided to hire me and what he and Barber were muttering about that day. I fully expected him to say something flattering about my voice. Instead, through a devilish smile, he said, "We hired you because you reminded us of Thomas Shippers."

Shippers had been the dashing operatic conductor with whom Menotti had an intimate relationship, until Shippers' untimely death at age forty-seven from lung cancer. Though it wasn't what I was expecting, I was still flattered … I guess. I didn't quite know how to respond and didn't pursue it. As I said, sometimes Menotti just liked to say something outrageous to see how you'd react.

The Spoleto Festivals

Il Festival dei Due Mondi—The Festival of Two Worlds—is a spectacular summer event with everything for the classic music lover. I was slated to sing Prince Yeletsky in *The Queen of Spades* with my buddy Jacque "Jack" Trussel. This was a wonderful opera for Jack, a superlative actor. The production provoked great enthusiasm, because it was the first year the festival was being held on American soil, as a counterpart to the Italian festival, which Gian Carlo Menotti had started in 1958.

The singers, instrumentalists, and sundry other staff were housed on a college campus right in the middle of Charleston, South Carolina. The city's white section was a pristine piece of the old South, except for automobiles and the power lines strung over the streets. Horse-drawn carriages carried Southern Belles to tea parties in their sun hats and long white dresses. It was like stepping into *Gone with the Wind*. I fully expected to bump into Rhett and Scarlett at any moment.

The festival was exceptional in every aspect. Christopher Keene, a marvelous pianist and Julius Rudel award winner from the early 1970s, was music director. He presided over a complex series of performances, from chamber music to opera and everything in between, in addition to his own orchestral rehearsals. I got to know him well during the festival, and I learned to appreciate his sardonic wit and riotous Menotti impression, which he performed at every opportunity.

Although my role was short, I had the best aria in *The Queen of Spades,* aka *Pique Dame.* This meant I had lots of free time to learn *Maria Golovin*—which I was to perform in Italy—and to work on my tan along the miles of deserted beach on Sullivan's Island. The shows were successful and well attended, and I got second glimpses of the festival's founder, but we didn't have any direct interactions.

When the American phase of the festival was complete, my wife and I immediately boarded a plane to Rome for the Italian festival. Most of the staff and a few of the other artists were involved in both festivals as well, so we all flew en masse. This was extremely convenient, because a group of Communist terrorists was wreaking havoc in Italy at the time, necessitating a lot of red tape to enter and exit the country. Police with submachine guns patrolled the airport, scrutinizing everybody. As members of the Menotti entourage, however, we were whisked through customs while the touristi stood in lengthy lines. Most of the group went directly to Spoleto, but we were taxied, with Menotti and a few close associates, to a beautiful hotel in the middle of Rome. During our short time there, I never saw a bill or paid for anything.

An hour later, I met Menotti and his staff in the lobby. We were driven to a beautiful building of Roman architecture, greeted in both English and Italian, and ushered to a small auditorium where I was seated in the front row next to Gian Carlo. What followed made me shockingly aware that my fluency in operatic Italian was almost useless in a conversational setting. My large vocabulary, most of it the Italian counterpart of Shakespearean English, had little relevance.

A dignified man with gray hair took the podium. He spoke extemporaneously for about twenty minutes. I understood almost nothing. I was a little frustrated; I had expected to comprehend more.

Then Menotti was invited to the stage. He spoke easily and fluently, and I understood some of what he was saying. I was relieved. He introduced me as the American baritone who would star in the revival of his opera. Then he sat down, and another person took the podium. I leaned in toward Menotti and whispered, "I couldn't understand a word that other man said."

"Ah yes, he's an actor and very self-impressed," he replied. "He uses very florid speech. Don't feel bad. Half the people in the room couldn't understand him."

I smiled but doubted him, because I couldn't understand what the others were saying, either. I realized that native Italians spoke very differently than Americanized Italians and was anxious to learn the difference. To be successful in this opera, I would have to sound like a native speaker.

On the way out, I stopped to use the sumptuous and elegantly designed men's room. As I stepped up to one of the urinals, I noticed it was unusually high. I assumed they were constructed either for very tall men or men with very short penises. Since neither situation applied to me, I moved to one of the marble and glass toilets, though they were so beautiful it seemed a shame to use them. But as I discovered, everything in Italy is meant to be a work of art—even a restroom.

I also noticed that nothing happens quickly in Italy, and rules are made to be broken. Apparently, during a postal strike some months before my arrival, the mail had piled up for weeks. Soon there was no room to store it, so the postal workers devised an innovative solution: They hauled the mail to a piazza and set it aflame. Problem solved. There were better things to do—like eat. And, boy, do the Italians know how to eat!

Menotti took us to lunch at a *trattoria* on the edge of the piazza that overlooks the magnificent Fontana di Trevi. I'd seen it many times on film, but no picture could capture the splendor of the incredible sculptures. As we sat there chatting in my pidgin Italian, I noticed two men on motor scooters cross the piazza, one in pursuit of the other. They came to a stop about twenty feet from us. The pursuer removed a tire iron from his scooter and swung it at the other man's head, connecting solidly. The victim fell, prostrate and bloody, holding his arms in a defensive posture. They shouted at each for several minutes. Then, as quickly as they appeared, both mounted their vehicles and drove away in opposite directions.

Nobody at the table seemed flustered except Menotti, who wondered if they should call the *polizia*. The others said it was no big deal, *non è niente*, and resumed eating as though nothing had happened. It occurred to me that the violence in American cities was perhaps not as distinct to our culture as the media would lead us to believe. Here, in the land of Leonardo, Michelangelo, Verdi, and Puccini, where the precepts of aestheticism and symmetry had been defined, it seemed incongruent. Then again, this was also the culture of Machiavelli, the de' Medicis, the Borgias, and the barbarism of the Roman Empire.

The next day we were driven to Spoleto, where my wife and I were escorted to a small apartment in the house of an Italian family. The sense of history was fabulous. The house was on an alley, *vicolo*, where Roman legions had marched. Aqueducts dating back to the seventh century still carried water across the mountain ridges. From our window, I could see the bridge from which Lucrezia Borgia had thrown her lovers to their deaths. And the walls that Hannibal assaulted in 218 B.C. still stood firm, separating Spoleto into two sections: Spoleto on the hilltop and Spoleto below. *Spoleto su e giu.*

Rehearsals started in earnest the next morning. Before we got under way, a cast member asked Menotti to explain his inspiration for the opera.

"When I was young," he said, "I was possessive. This is a story about jealousy and obsession."

Maria Golovin, much like his Pulitzer Prize-winning *The Consul*, contains some sinister and upsetting music—music that, in only a few strains, creates a tense sensation that delivers you into a perverse world of anguish and torment.

I played Donato, a tremendously challenging part. The character, a blind man, is onstage for all but ten minutes of the show. So, in addition to learning a long, complex part in very poetic Italian, I also had to persuade the audience that I was unable to see. I had my task cut out for me. This assignment would require elevating my skills to a new echelon.

The cast consisted of an American, a Brit, three Italians, and a Greek. The conductor, Christian Badea, was Romanian. Rehearsals were conducted in Italian, which I actually appreciated, because it forced me to learn theatrical vocabulary.

I was frequently translating for the British mezzo-soprano, who played the part of my mother. It was nice to have another Anglo around, with whom I could carry on a conversation involving more than "sit," "turn," and "cross to stage right."

There also were more egos on this show than one production could effectively contain. Fortunately, I was too overwhelmed with the assignment of learning the opera to be temperamental, so I constantly deferred to my colleagues. The conductor, a young man full of spice, was frustrated with the poor musicianship of the Italians. He played various musical tricks to see if he could trip them up. Then, when they made a mistake, he reprimanded them harshly. I was the only one who recognized his game and went along. He could never throw me off. A few years later, as the new music director of the National Symphony in Washington, D.C., Maestro Badea hired me to sing with the orchestra. We shared a mutual respect, if not a personal fondness for each other.

Menotti pushed the cast at a frantic rate. He sat in rehearsal with his bastone—a duplicate of the cane I was using as a prop—and banged it in on the floor when he saw or heard something he didn't like. Jumping to his feet, he'd shout in Italian, using quick, short sentences that were difficult to understand. I had no idea what he was saying most of the time, so I'd shrug, and follow my instincts. He rarely gave me directions during rehearsals.

Playing opposite me in the title role was Fiorella Carmen Forti, a former Italian celebrity of sorts. A successful singer and actress back in the late 1940s, she had appeared in films with Vittorio Gassman and Gina Lollobrigida. She retired after marrying a Greek shipping magnate. Sound familiar—a diva and a Greek tycoon?

Well, Callas and Onassis they were not. She was a much lesser diva and he a lesser shipping magnate. Nonetheless, rumor had it that the husband was footing the bill for the production as a means of jump-starting his wife's career.

Now, here she was, probably somewhere near sixty, not looking a day over forty—and a *good* forty at that—cast opposite a
thirty-year-old American baritone in the role of her lover. Yet it
was precisely what the libretto called for: a blind man bewitched
by a sophisticated older woman. In the story, Maria, accompanied
by her young son Trottolo, rents a room in the house Donato
shares with his mother. Maria is awaiting her husband's release
from a concentration camp but can't keep her legs together in
the meantime—a very Menotti-esque theme. With a cast of only
seven or eight, the complicated plot is tickled by an array of odd-
ball characters, most notably an escaped prisoner who has the best
line in the show: "One suffers less for the death of thousands, than
for the death of one."

Rehearsing in Italy, like eating in Italy, is an all-day affair. Rehearsals started at 10 a.m., six days a week, and frequently ran
until 10 p.m. with only a few breaks, including a two-hour siesta
beginning at noon. Being accustomed to America, where AGMA
artists may be rehearsed a maximum of six hours a day, I initially
found it difficult to adjust to this schedule. But once I got into
the flow, it became a very appealing way of life. An afternoon siesta breaks the day into two distinct halves and actually gives the
impression of having more time.

Menotti was a great stage director who made his job easier by
hiring exactly the right actors. He would block a scene like this:

"You start over here next to the table, stage right, and by the
time you sing this line, twelve pages later, you're over here by the
piano, stage left. Okay? Let's go."

For me, this was bliss. I was delighted he was not one of those
micromanaging narcissists who thought of singers as puppets
whose only reason for existence was to act out a highly controlled vision of their dream. With Menotti, I was free to explore
the character, to move how, when, and where I was motivated, as
long as I arrived at my destination at the appropriate time. This

requires you to do your homework and find constant motivation throughout the drama. Otherwise, you stand there, looking lost, waiting for your next musical cue.

Because the part was not vocally demanding, I could fill my moments onstage with the character's thoughts instead of thinking about The Voice. This allowed for a multi-layered characterization usually possible only in a play or film. With the added underscoring of the orchestra, the theatrical experience was breathtaking.

Maria and Donato shared a great number of love scenes—very sensual scenes with kissing and, since my character was blind, lots of touching as well. As an actor, I naturally assumed that we would really explore the intimacy of the scenes while we rehearsed. But Fiorella was from a different school of acting. The first time we had a love scene, she turned her head away as I started to kiss her. I assumed she was acting too, so I gently turned her face toward mine and kissed her. She went rigid for a moment and, with an embarrassed look on her face, turned her head so that we were cheek to cheek.

She whispered, "*Cattivo!*" Bad Boy!

Thereafter, whenever a kiss was indicated, she would try to pull away, all the while whispering, "*Cattivo! Cattivo!*" I didn't quite know what to think.

Finally, I approached Menotti and told him of my predicament.

He said, "Next time, grab her, kiss her, and don't let her go."

So I did. At the next kiss I grabbed her, planted one on her, and held tight. Her eyes opened wide as she tried to break my grasp. But she couldn't. When we finally broke the kiss, she stepped back and took a deep breath. Then half-staring, half-smiling, she exhaled audibly. We never had a problem with the kiss again.

Between rehearsals, Menotti would hold court. He loved to tell stories about his castle in East Lothian, Scotland, his retreat from the world. But despite this impressive piece of real estate, an aristocratic bearing, and his stature in the music world, the hearsay was that Menotti suffered from financial difficulties. Despite commissions from his many operas—especially *Amahl and the Night Visitors*, which is still the single most-performed work of its kind during the Christmas season—Menotti was essentially broke.

Unfortunately, opera composers are not remunerated like rock stars, and scuttlebutt had it that he was subsisting by way of a multi-year advance on his royalties from the G. Schirmer Inc. publishing house. I also noticed that Menotti rarely paid for anything. Somebody else always picked up the tab. And I would sometimes overhear fragments of whispered conversations about palazzos, secret benefactors, and princes of mysterious origin. He was a fascinating man.

During the last phase of rehearsals for *Maria Golovin*, everything started to come together. It looked as if we might actually have a show by opening night, but something wasn't quite right. I felt that my last line in the opera, an utterance of ultimate hatred and desperation, lacked the vocal power to match the emotions. So I went to Gian Carlo and said, "I've been experimenting with a higher ending. Can I show you what I have in mind?"

He looked at me in that odd way he had of not really looking at you and said, "Let's take a look at it."

He sat at the piano, patted the other end of the bench, and said slyly, "Sit."

I sat and pointed to a section of music with a pencil.

"I thought a high G here at the end would really pack a punch."

He took the pencil and languidly scratched a few notes. Then he said, "Hmmmm. What would you give me for a high G?"

Caught by surprise, I stammered, "Uh ... excuse me? Gi-give you...?"

I was unprepared for this. He, on the other hand, was highly amused by this cat-and-mouse game.

Trying to salvage a situation that I had never anticipated, I said, "Well, uh ... I could give ... a few lira ... a great performance, or maybe ... a bottle of wine? Or ... uh..."

Unable to come up with anything clever, and knowing full well what he was getting at, I said, "You know, maybe a high note here isn't such a good idea."

Then I reached for my score and started to get up, but Menotti held on to my wrist and chuckled, "You've been listening to rumors about me." And before I could answer, he added, "Well, they're all true."

With a flourish of his pen he notated alternate pitches in the score.

"There's your high G. Now you owe me a favor."

Still flustered, I said, "Done. Thank you," and got out of there as fast as I could.

My performances of *Maria Golovin* went marvelously. I received reviews praising my opulent voice, my perfect Italian, and my powerful acting, "which made it difficult," as one reviewer said, "to believe that he was not actually blind." One of the performances was taped and played on Italian television, and because opera singers are as beloved in Italy as sports stars are in America, I became a celebrity for a month.

Fiorella did not fare so well. Unkind reviews, together with some undisclosed conflict with Menotti, caused her to cancel the last performance and leave town in a huff—on her yacht.

It was a bittersweet end to a magnificent experience, like a chance erotic encounter with an exotic woman: You feel that mutual spark of magic during an intense moment of no-holds-barred passion, all the while knowing you will never—nor should ever—see each other again.

Despite my success, the words "Now you owe me a favor" kept running though my head. I knew it was unwise to make deals with the devil, because eventually he'll return to collect his due. I knew Menotti wasn't the devil, even though he enjoyed playing the role of a sinister rogue, but his words were hard to put out of my mind.

Sure enough, Gian Carlo would come back to collect on this particular debt. My bargain with him would lead to one of the most nightmarish experiences of my career—in the very same opera.

Holland

The rest of that year went smoothly, with engagements in and out of New York. Then one day the phone rang and Louise announced, "Menotti wants you to do *Golovin* in Holland."

I got a little tingle up my spine, but at the time I made light of it. Remember what I said before about learning to trust your instincts? Well, every nerve fiber was saying, *Don't take this gig!* But because I had made a deal with Gian Carlo, I ignored the warning.

The fees in the contract were lousy, something like five hundred American dollars per performance—a paltry sum, even by New York City Opera standards.

Performances were in the dead of winter, in the middle of a busy season at NYCO. This meant I would have to fly back and forth from New York to the Netherlands, and I'm not a particularly good traveler.

In addition, after having cancelled performances of the Count in *The Marriage of Figaro* at NYCO in two previous seasons, I was finally going to sing the damn thing. Although enthusiasm did not enter my range of emotions about the assignment, I had signed the contract and couldn't rationalize another cancellation.

The Count was a daunting role under any circumstances, but with the short rehearsal periods at NYCO, it was nerve-wracking. In ten leading roles there, only once did I see the set, wear the costumes, or actually hear the orchestra before stepping on the stage. Under most circumstances, this was no big deal. I was a master of "winging it." But in a complicated opera like *Figaro*, full of recitative, complex comic bits and some interminable ensembles, preparedness was vital. I didn't want to be distracted from this gargantuan task to relearn *Golovin* in English or make numerous trans-Atlantic flights in mid-season.

But Menotti was calling in his promise, and I, being an honorable man, accepted.

During a gap in the action at NYCO, I was scheduled to fly to Holland for a month to meet the company personnel, the cast, and do some rehearsals. This took place in Enschede, a small town on the Dutch-German border. Because I was not available for the first few performances, Menotti had hired a young British baritone to sing Donato, and I wondered why he hadn't just hired him for all of them. The cast was completely different from the cast in Italy, except for the role of Donato's Mother, which was again being beautifully portrayed by British mezzo-soprano Maureen Morelle.

I arrived at the remote outpost sometime in January and watched the last performance with the other baritone in my role. It was actually interesting to see it from the front for the first time. It helped me rethink a few difficult dramatic moments.

You never stop learning if you're doing it right.

The next day I was scheduled for my first rehearsal, and I arrived to find the conductor and pianist waiting in a large, cold rehearsal hall. We were alone. As it turned out, the other cast members, except for Maureen, were Americans living in Germany. They had driven home after the last performance, via the Autobahn, to fulfill other contracts. Maureen had taken the hovercraft across the English Channel and was no doubt as snug as a bug in a rug in her London flat.

Then I discovered that the conductor expected me to work

alone with him and a pianist in a dreary rehearsal hall for nearly a month—on an opera I already knew. I flipped. I came close to packing my bags and ditching the gig. But I was being paid by the week, and the company was picking up the tab for my room at a lovely little hotel not far away. Rationalizing that perhaps Enschede, like Amsterdam, could be a great place to hang out under the right circumstances, I resolved to stay.

That was mistake number one.

Then there was the Dutch penchant for smoking. They toke on pipes, cigarettes, cigars, and just about anything that can be lit. They smoke everywhere, all the time. When the pianist started to light up in the rehearsal room during a break, I went ballistic. They seemed baffled, even amused, when I tried to explain that I was allergic to smoke, and they would either cease and desist or requisition a gas mask from the prop room. To humor me, they posted notes around the facility stating that when Mr. Long was rehearsing, all smoking should be confined to the coffee room. Big deal! You had to come through the coffee room to get to the rehearsal rooms. But I figured if I took a running start as I entered the front door, I might be able to get through the smoky gauntlet without coughing up a lung.

And so the dreary days passed, until I made myself enough of a pain in the ass that everybody agreed further rehearsal was a waste of time. We took a hiatus until the rest of the cast arrived.

I spent the weekend of my thirtieth birthday sitting alone in an empty hotel eating cold cuts and fruit. It was some sort of Dutch holiday, and I was the sole guest at the hotel. The restaurant and bar downstairs were closed, and even the attractive redhead who worked the front desk was on vacation. At night I wandered the halls, playing scenes from *The Shining* in my head.

I dared not venture outside. Without a key to the hotel, I could be locked out, and they would find me on the doorstep imitating a Popsicle come Monday morning. I wished I'd had the good sense to go to Amsterdam for the weekend. Or better yet, the south of France.

Mercifully, just as I was about to jump over a dyke into the North Sea, the other cast members breezed into town, and we began the first set of performances. These didn't compare to the elating experiences I'd had in Italy. Not by a long shot. Ten minutes after singing my last note, I hailed a cab and was on my way to the airport, praying I could catch a plane to the good ol' U.S. of A. There was a two-week gap before I had to return to this frozen wasteland for one last performance in a little town called Groningen—a name that would forever be branded in my memory.

When I got back to New York, I had a few performances at NYCO. Then, in what seemed like no time at all, on a Wednesday night, I was headed back to Kennedy Airport to catch a red-eye to Amsterdam. The performance was on Friday, so I figured I had plenty of time to shake off the jet lag.

At that time, most flights heading across the Atlantic to Europe left at around 6 p.m., arriving at their European ports of call early the next morning. As usual, traffic out of Manhattan was terrible, and I missed my KLM flight. The only other possibility was on Air France, to Amsterdam via Paris. This was the beginning of a series of missed connections that ended in Hell.

I slept very little during the trans-Atlantic journey and arrived in Paris already exhausted. By the time I picked up my connection I was catatonic. I arrived in Amsterdam around 11 a.m. Thursday in an incoherent state. I'm a lousy traveler, but long west-to-east flights really knock the stuffing out of me.

Rather than try to get a train from Amsterdam to Groningen, I grabbed a taxi and told the driver to take me to a hotel where I could crash. By noon, I was checked into a quaint little place on one of Amsterdam's many waterways. Exhausted, I threw myself on the bed and did not budge until noon the next day.

When I awoke, I felt spacey and famished. Even the long sleep couldn't erase my overwhelming jet lag. Perhaps it had even made it worse. I was in a fog, outside of time and space, so I went out for a leisurely breakfast, with lots of caffeine, and then checked the train schedule. I would have preferred to spend the rest of the day tooling around Amsterdam, but I decided to head north in case of inclement weather. I packed and set off for the train station. The sun was out and I had a pleasant trip. I like train travel.

When I arrived in Groningen, I had no idea where to go. The company had not booked me a room, nor sent me a map of the city. Nor, in fact, had they contacted me in any way regarding the particulars of the performance. But this was a small town, so I figured, *How difficult can it be to find the theater?* Most Dutch people speak perfect English, usually with an American accent, so I'd ask for directions or take a cab.

I checked into a hotel next to the train station and proceeded to tour the picturesque little hamlet. I window-shopped, got a bite to eat, and made a splendid day of it. By happenstance, I came upon the theater and saw posters advertising *Maria Golovin*. I smiled as I read my name at the top of the cast list and noticed a truck unloading sets and costumes.

Hmmm, I pondered, *they're unloading a day early. How efficient the Teutonic races are.*

I walked right past the stage door with nary another thought.

On the way back to the hotel I saw a movie theater advertising a new American film release, *Smokey and the Bandit,* with Burt Reynolds and Sally Field.

Yes, a piece of Americana will make me feel better.

So I bought a ticket and went inside.

At movie theaters in Holland, patrons are escorted down the aisle by an usher and shown to an empty seat right beside somebody else, from the front to back of the theater. They pack 'em in, and God forbid they should waste a seat. I hated it. Americans like to spread out. We require more personal space than the Europeans.

Nonetheless, there I sat for two mindless hours watching Jackie Gleason chase Burt and Sally all over the southern highway system, reassured that America would still be there when I finished this ordeal.

The movie ended about 9 p.m., and I began a leisurely stroll back to the hotel, oblivious to everything around me except for the black sedan that pulled up on my left and stayed about ten feet behind me. This continued for a few blocks, and just as I was about to turn and confront my uninvited escort, I heard a British woman's voice say, "Charles? Charles, is that you?"

I squinted inside to see Maureen Morelle's familiar face, looking at me as though she'd seen a ghost. She opened the door and stepped from the car. The dome light illuminated the other cast members inside. I smiled.

"Hi, guys! What are you all doing here?"

Maureen looked at me, "What do you mean?"

"What are you all doing here a day early?"

Maureen hugged me tightly.

"Today is Friday," she whispered in my ear.

"No. It's Thursday ... isn't it?"

She slowly shook her head, "No, Charles, it's Friday. The performance was *tonight!*"

I stood there not really comprehending her words, my mind trying to grasp the concept, spinning in disbelief.

She continued, "When you didn't show up, the company called KLM and discovered that you were not on your scheduled flight, but immigration told them that you had indeed entered the country. Then they started calling the police and the hospitals. Thank God you're all right. What happened?"

Then it all started to fall into place. My flight left New York at 6 p.m. Wednesday and arrived in Amsterdam Thursday morning. Then I slept for a disoriented twelve hours and awoke on Friday, thinking it was still Thursday. I never experienced Thursday, because I slept through it. With the time change and my extreme disorientation, I had completely lost track of the days, my brain picking up where it left off before I did my Rip Van Winkle imitation.

I joined my colleagues in the car, and while I tried to explain, they, I think, were trying to determine whether I was drunk or on drugs. On the drive back to my hotel they filled in the rest of the story: When I didn't show up for a half-hour, everybody started getting nervous. They called KLM, then immigration, and started to call around to some of the hotels. As time passed, it was obvious I was nowhere to be found. The show-must-go-on guarantee became impossible. The only other person who knew my part was sitting in London, hours away, even by plane. So they paid all the performers, refunded tickets, and sent the audience home. Unbelievable!

With expressions of compassion, my colleagues dropped me off at my hotel. Maureen hugged me again and urged me to take care of myself, but I'd already fallen into a delirium, so I just nodded and waved over my shoulder. I trundled up to my room and lay on my bed all night staring at the ceiling, running the events over and over in my mind. But it was done. There was no going back to fix it. I had committed the unthinkable—I had actually missed a performance.

As dawn approached, I had no idea how to handle the situation, but I knew one thing for certain—I had to get the hell out of Dodge. I grabbed my bags and took the first train to Amsterdam, then a shuttle to the airport. Once I was at the gate, ready to board, I called the company manager.

When he recognized my voice he groaned, "Mr. Long. What happened?"

I quickly said, "Look I'm dreadfully sorry about this, but I'm on my way back to New York. Last night was a major fuck-up, so I owe you. Determine the cost of last night's performance, and I'll come back and sing an opera of your choice, free of charge, based upon my U.S. fee. This, of course, can be negotiated."

All he could do was mutter, "Mr. Long, Mr. Long, Mr. Long."

My heart went out to him, but there was nothing more to say. I improvised the best offer I could think of to help him recoup the lost revenue.

I boarded the plane and as it ascended, I cursed Odin, Thor, and any Norse god within earshot for having invoked this bloody nightmare. Then I recanted. At least they were letting me get away before the thunderbolts struck.

I didn't hear anything for months. Then, one day a letter from an attorney in the Netherlands arrived. It requested that I pay the sum of something like a bazillion Dutch guilders for my non-appearance in Groningen. I asked Louise to make another offer for a series of free performances, but we never heard from them again.

I didn't see Gian Carlo Menotti until the next summer, again at the Spoleto Festival in Charleston. During a break in my schedule I decided to swing by his rehearsal and say hello. When I walked into the room, Menotti jumped up from his chair, stopping the rehearsal, and in an exaggerated style shouted, "Here he is! He's arrived!"

Grabbing his assistant director he said, "Make sure he gets a call the night of ALL his performances. We don't want to take any chances." Then he laughed his characteristic Menotti laugh, abruptly returned to his chair and continued the rehearsal without skipping a beat.

We never spoke of the incident. That was his way of giving me good "gotcha" and leaving it alone. I must say, however, that my missed performance story was the buzz of the festival for weeks.

❧ *Accelerando*

❧ When Opportunities Knock

Being at the right place at the right time has opened more doors than any other path into show business. Be prepared for the unexpected, and opportunity will knock.

I enjoyed a number of these strokes of good fortune in my day. Lady Luck smiled upon me on my way up the ladder, and she left me forsaken on the way down. But, in true Darwinian fashion, these cycles of life and death provide opportunities for others. Like predators of the wild that pounce on the weak, ill, and unaware, so too in the world of men must we climb over the corpses of the fallen—if we are to rise above the fray. It's not an existence for the faint of heart or the overly scrupulous. If you're not ready to stand and trade punches with those who would usurp your territory, you'll go home on your shield—and few, especially the circling buzzards, will mourn your passing.

Shortly after my debut at NYCO, I was given the assignment of covering Tonio in *Pagliacci*, a role I knew well. The production was staged by Frank Corsaro, a marvelously innovative director, and it involved a more intricate staging than one usually sees. Rather than depend on the minimal hours of rehearsal normally provided for covers, I attended the opening cast's rehearsals, making mental notes of the stage directions in my mind. I was very conscientious.

One night I arrived to sing Alfio in *Cavalleria Rusticana*, and no sooner had I started my makeup than the stage manager and the assistant director popped their heads in and asked how I was feeling.

"Great!" I said.

"Glad to hear it," the AD announced. "Dick is ill. You're doing both operas tonight."

Cavalleria Rusticana and *Pagliacci*, abbreviated Cav/Pag, are one-act operas often done in the same evening on a double bill. Sometimes the same tenor does sing both operas, though the soprano rarely does and only occasionally does the baritone. Yet here I was, with only two seasons at NYCO under my belt, being given this unusual assignment with little rehearsal. These were the kinds of experiences that could make a man of you—*if* you could pull it off.

Richard Fredricks was the baritone I replaced that night. Dick was a snooty, aloof guy. He was tall and elegant, handsome in a stern way, with a beautifully trimmed beard that he refused to shave for any reason. Though many people around the opera house thought Dick was a dick, I liked him. We developed an easy rapport. We even became what might be described as chummy, which was convenient since we were sharing a dressing room for this double bill.

Dick had a reliable voice, and he was the house baritone of that period. Unlike most of the other soloists, he was on a weekly contract, and his name could be seen on the playbill frequently. I don't think there was a baritone role in the repertory he didn't sing at some point during his tenure. But despite his rigorous schedule, many people suspected that Dick Fredricks was not totally dedicated. He acted more like a dilettante than somebody seriously pursuing a career.

I'm not saying he wasn't a talented artist. He was. And he certainly was competitive. It's just that he never appeared to be passionate about it. He talked of flying his plane, or investing in California real estate, or things unassociated with show business. In later years, I would learn to admire Dick Fredricks's detachment.

Fortunately, my friend Cal Kellogg was conducting that night. Our friendship was enhanced by a strong musical kinship. He had been a bassoonist and I an oboist, so we inevitably shared stories that only double-reed players seem to know. As I applied my makeup and donned my costume for *Cavalleria*, Cal and I hummed our way through *Pagliacci*, stopping only to share crucial musical information.

I went onstage and sang Alfio, interpolating a high G-sharp at the end of my aria, just to test it. It felt great. I was ready.

Immediately after curtain calls I raced backstage where dressers tore my clothes off, and makeup artists started on a new face. Tonio sings the opening lines to *Pagliacci* as a prologue to the audience before the curtain rises. I had only a short time to transform from the wealthy Sicilian in *Cavalleria* to the vengeful hunchback in *Pagliacci*.

When the transformation was complete, I walked to the stage and stood behind the curtain, listening to the familiar opening strains of "Il Prologo." I was amazed at my composure. I don't think my heart rate ever exceeded seventy-two. There was no time to be nervous. I took a deep breath, as two stagehands pulled the curtains apart, and I stepped into the spotlight, squinting out at the State Theater's thirty-two-hundred seats. I sang the Prologue for all I was worth and received a spectacular ovation. The rest of the opera flew by, and I have very little recollection of it.

The next day, John White, the general manager, called me into his office. He gave me congratulations and a bonus check. I had arrived—and man, did it feel great!

A short time later, Dick and I were scheduled to sing Cav/Pag again and, as was customary, we shared a dressing room. He was already at his makeup table when I arrived. Never looking away from the mirror, he asked me how I had done in *Pagliacci*.

"I did well."

"How was the A-flat in the Prologue?" he asked.

"It was great!" I said.

"Fuck you!"

We both laughed. But it was a tense laughter. Until that moment I had been the young apprentice who presented no threat. But now I had made my mark at his expense, and our relationship changed. Though we acknowledged each other and nodded greetings, we never really spoke again. And so it goes…

When Lawrence Tibbett was the reigning baritone at the Met, a young singer named Leonard Warren, the heir apparent, was scheduled to sing Ford to Tibbett's Falstaff. Tibbett himself had climbed to prominence playing Ford to Antonio Scotti's Falstaff in 1925, and he had no intention of giving the young hotshot a similar opportunity. He politicked to have the casting changed, but other powers at the Met prevailed. Warren capitalized on the opportunity and usurped Tibbett's throne.

But Lady Luck can turn a cold cheek, reclaiming in an instant all she has bestowed. Leonard Warren dropped dead of a cerebral hemorrhage at age forty-eight, at the height of his career, during a Met performance of *La Forza del Destino*—*The Force of Destiny*. What irony.

Not too long after my double-bill success, the production of *Fanciulla del West* I had performed in Houston and Miami was finally scheduled at NYCO. Veteran Bill Chapman, who bounced between opera and musical theater, was scheduled to sing Jack Rance. I liked Bill very much; he was a real sweet guy. But *Fanciulla* is a complicated opera, and Bill was no musician. I had witnessed Julius Rudel practically tear Bill's heart out in a full-cast rehearsal of *Carmen* one day when he had been musically sloppy. *Carmen* is a cakewalk compared to the sinewy textures and constantly changing meters of *Fanciulla*. So I lobbied to be Bill's understudy and got the gig. Then I just sat back and waited—like a lion on the savanna.

It was rumored that Bill had a rather severe drinking problem, although I never saw him intoxicated. This problem was said to become worse as opening night approached, so I steered clear of rehearsals until the Thursday before dress rehearsal. When I dropped in, I saw Frank Corsaro and the conductor, Sergui Comissiona, struggling to keep Bill afloat. I took Frank aside and told him not to worry. I assured him I knew the part like the back of my hand. Then I wished them all well and made a hasty exit.

Two days later, while I was sipping my morning tea, Frank called. "Can you come and do the dress rehearsal today and the opening Saturday?"

"I'll be right there, Frank," I replied, and calmly walked the ten blocks from my apartment to Lincoln Center.

Once again, dressers and makeup artists pinned me into costumes made for somebody else, while Corsaro talked me through the staging. With the exception of a couple of wrong crosses, to which everybody adapted, it went without a hitch, as did the premiere the next night with Ermano Mauro and Marilyn Niska. A photo of the three of us in the poker game scene in Act II appears in the City Opera Book. There I am in Bill Chapman's wig and costume, three sizes too large. It always makes me laugh—and cry a little bit, too.

As a punctuation to this story, the second performance of *Fanciulla* was scheduled a week later. I picked up a cold somewhere, which became laryngitis. I used every medication at my disposal, but it was right on my vocal cords, and I knew I was in trouble. I alerted the company, but with Bill out of the picture, there was no cover. I agreed to go on. The office found a guy who knew the part, a baritone who was covering roles next door at the Met that season, and arranged to have him in the theater.

Though I made a noble attempt, I had no voice at all by the end of the first act. Julius Rudel came backstage and urged me to continue, but I couldn't even speak by then, let alone sing.

In retrospect, I should have done anything to get through it. Instead, my cover went on, just as I had gone on for Fredricks and Chapman.

Unbeknownst to me, my cover had squeezed NYCO hard. He demanded a substantial fee and a guarantee for the bulk of future performances of *Fanciulla*. So, as quickly as I was in, I was out, having to settle for the scraps of the remaining performances. It taught me a harsh lesson: Don't get cocky, and be merciless in your negotiations. Nobody will look out for you, if you don't look out for yourself.

I was growing up. But I wasn't sure that I liked what I was becoming.

It's Always *Rigoletto*

My next opportunity came out of nowhere. I was in Boston visiting a soprano with whom I was involved at the time. She was singing *Hansel and Gretel* with the infamous Sarah Caldwell.

Ours was a very combative relationship, but I was recently separated and had no place better to go—my wife having gotten the apartment. It was the middle of winter, but Boston seemed as good as anywhere else.

My flame and I were having an unpleasant time of it, when my manager called with an offer to fly down to West Palm Beach to replace a NYCO colleague, Dominic Cossa, as Rigoletto that night. It was a reprieve, surely sent from Heaven. I would get to leave this cold place, this icy shrew, and make a few bucks singing one of my favorite operas—ironically, the same opera in which the shrew and I had met.

Frantic negotiations ensued, and we quickly agreed on a fee. I strong-armed them for a guarantee of both performances, regardless of Dom's improvement. This was not comfortable for me, but

I had learned to play hardball during NYCO's *Fanciulla*, and I was determined to use leverage to my advantage this time. They were reluctant to make the deal, but they were in a bind, and I was their salvation. They had no choice. I boarded a plane to South Florida that afternoon.

A limo met me at the airport and drove me to the theater, where the cast was already assembling. I improvised some makeup out of whatever I could borrow, donned my costume, and walked to the stage. The conductor approached me in a tizzy. I assured him that I'd watch him like a hawk, and all would be well.

"Hey, It's only *Rigoletto*," I said, laughing at my private joke. This brought an uncomfortable look, but I didn't care. He already disliked me because of the contract negotiations, so I had nothing to lose.

I walked over to the girl playing the role of my daughter, shook her hand and said, "Do whatever you've been doing, I'll be there. This is going to be fun."

And I must say it was one of the smoothest performances of *Rigoletto* I ever sang. Actually, from an actor's standpoint, there were moments of magic. The other singers did what they had rehearsed, while I worked around them, adding elements of improvisation and spontaneity. It was marvelous.

At the end of the gig they let me know, quite unceremoniously, that holding them ransom for the second performance had been unprofessional. They said, "You sang beautifully. Here's your check. You'll never be asked back."

Wow, this is getting to be a trend.

But hey, if I wasn't going to be reengaged when I was a nice guy, as I had been so many times in the past, then why not be a prick? At least pricks get respect. Look at John McEnroe. I'd get my paydays and cover my ass. And if I pissed off everybody in America, there was always Europe—except for Holland, that is.

Sing, Herman! Sing!

As I've mentioned, budgetary concerns at New York City Opera created a situation where preparation was minimal at best and nonexistent at worst. One of my colleagues, a stalwart tenor by the name of Herman Malamood, had been a member of the NYCO family for many years. But he had seen better days and was soon expected to sing his swan song, as more formidable talents blossomed from the ranks below.

Every new season at NYCO was like the spring planting. You could see the fertile ground burgeoning with life, and it was anybody's guess which seedlings would pop their little heads through the soil and emerge as man-eating plants. It was a lot like the musical *Little Shop of Horrors*.

This particular season, Herman was scheduled to sing Canio in the opening performance of *Pagliacci*. His cover was Kenneth Riegel, an up-and-comer who was singing *Turandot*, among other operas, and with the additional task of covering *Pagliacci*, he really had his hands full.

Because this was the opening night for Cav/Pag, all covers were required to be in the house. Most of us sat in the company box watching the performance. The box contained about twenty seats, in two rows, stuffed into a little nook at the rear of the orchestra section. I was covering both Alfio and Tonio that evening, so I plunked myself down in the back row and prepared for a long, boring night.

Cavalleria played, and during intermission many of the covers went home. The ones remaining were the diehards and those required to stay for *Pagliacci*. As the opening strains to the Prologue began, I noticed Ken Riegel sneak into the darkened box and sit at the end of my row, nonchalantly flipping through his score as he fidgeted in his seat.

Hmmm, I thought. *It's opening night and he's still on the score?*

The lights dimmed.

Pablo Elvira, a good-natured Mexican baritone, was singing Tonio. He did a nice job on the Prologue, and the audience applauded in appreciation as the curtain rose. The chorus swirled around the stage as the action moved into the opening scene. Herman Malamood sang his first entrance, sounding just as expected. Solid. No frills.

As the scene went on, however, I thought I heard a few pops and clicks in his voice and a decline in volume. A few people in the box exchanged quick glances, shrugged, and then turned back to the stage. In all his years, Herman had never cancelled a performance. Reliability was his middle name. Surely he just had some phlegm.

But as Herman started into his little aria at the end of the scene, it became apparent that the clicks and pops were more serious. Something was clearly wrong. As any cover can tell you, this causes pins and needles to run through your body, and a heightened sense of awareness takes hold. Even if you're not the one with your ass on the line, you get a vicarious jolt of kill-or-be-killed adrenaline.

Now, even in the dim, reflected light from the stage, I could see a trickle of sweat roll down Ken's forehead. His mouth was ajar and his eyes wide, like the proverbial deer in the headlights. He opened his score and quickly shuffled through the pages, looking back and forth from the music to the stage, panic overrunning his features. Every head in the box now turned toward Ken Riegel with the kind of fascination people have when they gawk at an accident on the highway. It's irresistible.

Meanwhile, onstage, Herman's voice had crumbled into nothing more than a croak, and the audience became very aware of it. The orchestra played, Herman croaked, and time stood still. Suddenly the door at the back of the box flew open. The assistant stage manager ran up the steps, spotted Ken, grabbed him by the collar, and pulled him out the door. The rest of us murmured and gesticulated frantically, touching faces in variations of hear no evil, see no evil, speak no evil.

A quick huddle ensued, as we began placing bets on the out-come—all in the spirit of good fun, of course. It was ragged odds on two solutions: Would they put Ken in Herman's costume and throw him onstage and to the wolves, or would they have Ken sing offstage while Herman mimed the part? The latter was the heavy favorite, but somebody threw in a 10-to-1 bet they'd get on the phone and try to find a tenor who knew the part. Maybe. But it was a long shot.

During all this, the soprano sang her aria, then her duets with the two baritones. I sensed that the conductor was taking every-thing at the slowest possible tempo, to give whomever time to do whatever. But since it was a one-act opera with no intermissions, he was clueless to the backstage drama.

We all waited in breathless anticipation as the Nedda-Silvio love duet ended with the words, "*t'amo, t'amo, t'amo.*"

I looked around at the expressions of my colleagues and thought: *This must have been the look in the eyes of the Roman mob at the Coliseum, as they gazed onto the bloody sand below, while the gates to the gladiatorial chamber slowly opened…*

Two figures, not gladiators but Tonio and Canio, crept onstage behind the lovers, and as they stepped out into the light I saw that Herman was one of them. But as soon as he opened his mouth to sing, a disconnected voice that was not his came from … where?

Oh, my God, it was coming from the orchestra pit! They had put Ken Riegel right next to the conductor, score in hand, and he was reading the part. Since it was not exactly a scenario anybody had anticipated, all bets were off.

This is one of the reasons live theater is so exciting, and now the audience was actually getting caught up in the whole drama.

Earlier, while we had enjoyed a game of chance at the expense of our colleagues' careers, Herman's wife—by reputation a truly daunting stage wife—had pushed her way backstage to find out what was happening. She positioned herself in the wings, stage left, from where she was now hissing words of encouragement to her husband. Meanwhile, Ken Riegel was singing pretty damn well, even though he was buried down in the pit, miles away from the action on the stage. The better Ken sang, the louder Herman's wife hissed.

The music moved into the famous aria "Vesti la Giubba," and the evening took on the improvisational qualities of one of those off-off-Broadway performance-art exhibitions that frequently play in the West Village. Alone on stage and getting into the theatrics of the moment, Herman began to speak his lines over the voice of Ken Riegel in the pit. As the music approached the immortal phrase "*Ridi, Pagliaccio*," Herman's wife screamed from the wings, "Sing, Herman! Sing!" And with what was left of his broken voice, Herman sang. The two tenors simultaneously began the final eight bars of the most famous tenor aria in all of opera.

At the end, the audience sat dumbfounded, unsure of whether they should applaud or crawl under their seats. It was like the "Springtime for Hitler" scene in the Mel Brooks film *The Producers*.

An intermezzo occurred before the next scene, and one can only imagine what went on in the dressing room. Whatever transpired, Herman repressed any further impulse to sing. And to his credit, Ken remained tastefully silent in the closing moments of the opera, allowing Herman to speak the final line, "*La comedia e finita!*"

Truer words were never spoken.

Those of us in the box left the theater knowing we had seen an unrepeatable event. I walked home pensively and had disturbing dreams that night. I suffered a little for both singers and prayed such a thing would never happen to me.

So much for the power of prayer.

The next day was our dark night, but while I was out and about I took a swing by the theater to check the rehearsal schedule. The day's page was blank except for a four-hour slot marked in red: "Riegel. Pagliacci, Music and Staging."

Talk about closing the barn door after the horse has run off.

🐚 Mental Preparation

Learning an operatic role is a long, demanding process, even for somebody with an instrumental background.

You start by buying a score containing the vocal lines over a piano reduction of the orchestration. After highlighting your own lines with a yellow marker, so you can quickly go from cue to cue, you read through it a number of times to get a sense of the part.

If the piece is in a foreign language—by no means uncommon in opera—you begin by breaking the sentences into words you can understand. You analyze the meter, the phrases, and mark the places where you need to take your breaths. Then you go to the piano, or to a coach, and painstakingly add melody to those lyrics.

Understanding the nuances of another language requires immeasurable patience. Nothing is more painful than hearing a colleague sing Italian with an American accent. British accents are even worse. But sometimes even native speakers have difficulties performing in their own language.

I remember Menotti correcting Fiorella Carmen Forti when we were rehearsing *Maria Golovin*. Coming from southern Italy, her vowels were very closed, which is anathema in lyrical Italian. Every time she sang the words "*solo a te,*" pronouncing them, "*sulu ah tee,*" Menotti would stomp his feet and bang his cane in frustration, pronouncing the words for her, again and again. "*No! Solo a te! Solo a te!*"

It's hard enough being ridiculed for your pronunciation of a foreign language, but to be chastised for the way you speak your mother tongue … ouch! No wonder she left town.

To work an opera into The Voice and really make it your own is a months-long process. Not only do you have to learn the words, pitches, rhythms, dynamics, and the accompaniment, but you must also learn all of your cues and internalize the flow of the scenes—including the scenes in which you're not involved.

Most of the time, the first stages of this learning process are so intimidating that you fear you'll never be able to memorize it. Yet there are some rare instances when an opus just falls into you, like a lover whose proportions so perfectly match yours that, from the first, it feels as though you were meant to be together.

For years, I had been fascinated with Robert Ward's opera *The Crucible*, which closely follows Arthur Miller's play. The role of John Proctor always spoke to me. I had obsessed about the part. I related to the character of a man of such deep principles that he was unable to bow to the powers that assailed him, even at the cost of his own life.

I had learned bits and pieces of *The Crucible* in a workshop early in my career. But the opera was rarely produced, so I never had a chance to see it. It was one of those operas I listened to when I wanted to be inspired. I would often play the recording while watching the score and hum along. The melodies would stay with me for days, running in the background noise of my mind. There they would remain, until I started to learn something else.

One day Moritz Bomhard, general director of Kentucky Opera, where I'd had successes in *Rigoletto* and *Il Trovatore*, asked me if I'd like to do anything that might be within his budget. Immediately, I said *The Crucible*. He loved the idea and, because it's a small-scale opera, he was able to sell it to the board of directors.

So, in the midst of an enormously busy season, I was to have my shot at John Proctor. But with three other operas to learn, I had no time to study it. I carried the musical score with me as I traveled around the country, but I never once found the opportunity to open it.

Singing in Louisville was always like a homecoming. I'd received one of my first big breaks in that charming town, so I was relatively certain I'd be given some latitude if I didn't have the music completely internalized by the time I arrived. I also knew the conductor, Judy Somogi, from the old days when she had been assistant chorus master at NYCO. The director was unknown to me, but I had heard good things about her.

Something remarkable happened at the first rehearsal. I placed my score on a music stand and prepared to open it, but a voice in my head said, *Stop! You don't need the music.*

It was like that moment in *Star Wars* when Luke Skywalker prepares to launch his torpedo down the intake tube of the Death Star and the spirit of Obi-Wan Kenobi whispers, "Use the Force, Luke!"

The voice in my head was right. It was an authentic "may the force be with you" moment. I sang the rehearsal flawlessly without ever referring to the score. Through some kind of osmosis, over a ten-year period, I had absorbed the role without studying it in my traditional way. I had never done that before and never since.

Playing John Proctor was an intensely cathartic experience. As an actor, I had always been able to separate myself from the emotion, to put on whatever mask was required and still be entirely believable. But some things in *The Crucible* hit so close to home that I couldn't employ the detachment I'd learned in acting class. In one scene, Elizabeth confronts John about his fornication with Abigail, and John cries, "Judge me not. Let you look to your own improvement! I've forgotten Abigail!"

Singing that passage, I actually suffered the agony of the confrontation, because I had experienced it in my own life. I felt John's white-hot anger, his hopeless anguish, and his shame over his lie to everyone and to himself.

In every performance, at the end of the courtroom scene, when all assembled scream at the top of their voices, "John Proctor's the Devil's man!" I felt an odd tingling paralysis in the fingers of both hands. I couldn't shake it. It was autonomic and frightening.

In the final scene, as John is led to the gallows for refusing to sign a confession, I lost all sense of consciousness as I knew it. By the time I became aware of my surroundings again, the show was over and somebody was pushing me out for a curtain call.

As an atheist, nothing about this experience changed my beliefs about deities and demons; but the power of this drama overwhelmed me with an onstage reality unlike anything I'd ever known. I played the part, and I loved it … at least, I think I did. But I'm not sure I could survive doing it again.

🖎 Amsterdam versus Kennedy Center

"Be impeccable with your word."
The Four Agreements
—Don Miguel Ruiz

This has always been an important ethical premise for me. My grandmother infused me with an ironclad sense of honor, and I can say with all humility that the times I have betrayed this self-imposed pledge can be counted on the fingers of one hand. But, alas, I'm human, and there have been occasions when I've not lived up to my ideals.

During my career, I prided myself on the fact that when I signed a contract for a gig, I honored that contract—even when a tastier carrot dangled in front of my nose. A handshake was as good as a blood oath, and my word was gold. However, I did falter once.

I was becoming a very busy baritone with a string of huge

successes. Everything seemed to be going my way. I was recently divorced, and a fiery new relationship inspired me. I found myself in a completely unfamiliar situation—one of receiving multiple offers for the same time period. I could pick and choose roles for the first time in my career. I no longer had to take any job that was offered. I was in such demand that my manager set companies against each other bidding for my services. It felt great.

After the humiliation of countless auditions, and my negative experiences in San Francisco and Houston, to be suddenly in demand was hugely reassuring.

For example, I was offered a contract to sing Tonio in *Pagliacci* at Holland National Opera. Like most European contracts, it involved numerous performances, and though the per-performance fee was low by American standards, by the end of the run I would have amassed a considerable sum. I was not eager to be in Holland during winter again—or at all, for that matter—fearing Interpol might be waiting for me after my last Netherlands escapade. Nonetheless, after much consideration, I accepted the contract.

Then, out of nowhere, Frank Rizzo of Washington Opera called.

"We're mounting a production of *Tosca* for Shirley Verrett and Carlo Bergonzi," he said. "John Mauceri would like you to sing Scarpia."

I was flabbergasted—not only by the suddenness of such an offer but also because I'd experienced a bumpy past with Maestro Mauceri. We first worked together at NYCO in *La Bohème* and clashed once or twice about inconsequential musical preferences. I saw him as an inexperienced, preppie conductor who was a bit too literal for Puccini, and I'm sure he thought I was a jerk, too. But, even in those early years, John showed the signs of a consummate political creature. He knew whom to wine and dine and whose ass to kiss, and he was brilliantly skilled at networking. It must have been that Ivy League education.

A good while passed before our paths crossed again, after I'd done a production of Donizetti's little-known opera *Il Furioso all'isola di San Domingo* at one of the Spoleto festivals. It was an extremely difficult part but, ultimately, a wild success. The structure of the music and the madman drama lent itself to all sorts of interpolated high notes, and I'd taken full advantage—so much so that a tenor colleague came backstage after one of the shows and said, "It was incredible! You sounded like a baritone Corelli."

High praise, indeed!

But I digress.

A year after the Spoleto production, *Il Furioso* was brought to the Kennedy Center in Washington, D.C., and John Mauceri was the conductor. I was retained as Cardenio, as was the director, Richard Perlman. The rest of the cast were all different.

The music had been "reworked" by musicologist and critic Andrew Porter. A few keys were changed, a duet extended here, a note tweaked there; this reversed, that turned upside down—just enough alteration to be really annoying.

I've always mocked musicologists, and I despise most critics, so here was Andrew Porter, an obsequious Brit who was *both*, and therefore, in my estimation, devoid of any redeeming qualities. I rarely agreed with his reviews, and he'd made such a mess of *this* work that an already disjointed opera became even more confusing. Add to that the fact he had once given me a not-so-flattering review, and I had the makings of one dandy chip on my shoulder.

Unfortunately, he'd also written the best English translations of the Verdi operas I'd ever read, so I had to cut the guy some slack.

As an aside, Porter and I worked together again in Seattle years later, when he directed *La Forza del Destino*. He wasn't half-bad, and I developed a new respect for him. It's one thing to study a composer's work, write lofty opinions about it, and attack artists who have the balls to do it. It's another thing entirely to go out on the limb and do it yourself. I admired him for trying.

But back to John Mauceri and the Kennedy Center production of *Il Furioso*.

In addition to all the undercurrents of this production, I was going through marital problems, suffering from allergies, and felt generally in a funk. Rehearsals were trying. I was temperamental and doing a wonderful job of alienating my colleagues, especially John, with my unflattering and unsolicited comments about the musical changes. Although the performances brought me critical acclaim, Mauceri and I parted on less-than-congenial terms. Naturally, I assumed our paths would never cross again.

Sometime later, baritone Juan Pons canceled his contract to sing *L'Amore dei Tre Re* at the John F. Kennedy Center in Washington. At the eleventh hour, they asked me to come in and save the day. Mauceri was the conductor, and I heard he had implored the company not to hire me. He didn't want to contend with my foul humor again, and I didn't blame him. Yet I had the advantage of being one of the few baritones who could learn an entire opera, in Italian, and have it performance-ready in five days. The opera company sent me the score and a tape. As I was between apartments at the time, I went to my parents' house in Pittsburgh, sat at the piano I had played as a teenager, and learned the role of Manfredo.

Less than a week passed, and I walked into rehearsal at the Kennedy Center without the score—mostly to show John I wasn't as big a jerk as he thought, but also to remind him he was dealing with a highly skilled artist who was on his way up and he shouldn't fuck with me.

I was really on for those performances, and the reviews, even from *Washington Post* critic Paul Hume, a renowned slayer of singers—including Harry Truman's daughter, Margaret—couldn't have been better if my mother had written them.

Now, fast-forward to Washington Opera's offer for the role of Scarpia.

I was being offered my favorite role, among a stellar cast at the Kennedy Center, when I had already contracted for the other engagement in Holland. By signing a contract, I had given my word and, though others sneered at me for having such scruples, the pledge meant something to me. And even though the job was still three months in the future, Hans de Roo had come all the way to the United States, held auditions, and was eager to have me sing with his company. This was an ideal opportunity to return to the Netherlands on far better terms than I had left.

What to do?

Remarkably, the Kennedy Center complicated things further by offering to bump my fee to cover any shortfall I might experience from giving up three months of work in Holland.

At that point I thought: *Why am I being so loyal to a business where almost everyone is self-serving, and most people can't even define the word 'scrupulous?'*

This jovial young man from western Pennsylvania had come a long way—from trusting optimist to hardened cynic. That part was sad. But such was the ante for the game.

Louise canceled the job in Amsterdam, and I recommended a friend to replace me. I signed the *Tosca* contract, and it was one of the best decisions I ever made. The *Tosca* was a resounding success and began a mutual admiration society between me and superstar Shirley Verrett, a colleague who renewed my faith in mankind. She requested me as her Scarpia numerous times over the following years. I became recognized as one of the important interpreters of the role, even having my own costume, wig, and special props made. My *Tosca* score, my costume and wig, along with an autographed photo of me with Shirley are some of the few things I have kept as sentimental reminders of those years.

Shirley had to cancel her final Kennedy Center performance because of terrible allergies, and a gal from New York was flown in. My friend Cal Kellogg, who was in town conducting

Washington Opera's *Falstaff*, sat in the prompter's box and threw cues to her while we improvised our way through the performance, bringing an odd closure to a dream job.

Though I ended things with John Mauceri on pretty good terms, we never worked together again. He accumulated some impressive accomplishments thereafter, and twenty-five years after that glorious production of *Tosca*, I once dropped him an email.

He never replied.

Well, fuck me!

❧ The Smell of the Greasepaint

Charles Elsen was a tenor in the regular chorus at NYCO when I first met him. His extraordinary makeup skills caught everyone's attention. An artist whose canvas was the human face, Charles could change a troll into a prince or a double-chinned diva into Cleopatra. Under his carefully applied layers of gradual shading, the transformations were astonishing.

His own makeup was so remarkable that one's eye went to him immediately when he walked onstage. Soloists who craved more of the spotlight were the first to notice, quickly snubbing the company makeup staff and engaging Charles to do it instead. Soon, all the headliners were gladly spending the extra bucks to look a whole lot better, and what had been a hobby became a lucrative vocation. The word spread, and over the next few years Charles Elsen trained a troupe of artists in his techniques, and they traveled from one company to another, providing wigs and makeup.

Elsen Associates usually showed up a few days before dress rehearsal, and immediately the fun began. Charles was among the most outrageous of gay men in an already outrageous industry. This was somewhat surprising, because if you were to engage him in casual conversation or see him walking on the street, you would not necessarily label him a homosexual. But in the comfort of his own milieu he was a flaming fag—and entertaining to the extreme.

Heterosexuals usually manage to integrate their sexuality into the fabric of their lives. The fact that one is straight doesn't usually come up in the course of daily conversation. But gay men tend to define themselves, and every aspect of their lives, through their sexual orientation. Every thought, expression, and opinion is colored with the pastels of their gaiety. It almost seems that once society gave them permission to come out of the closet, they were determined to flaunt their "I am what I am" declaration in the loudest voice possible.

I had become accustomed to all this after many years in the business, but Charles brought a unique twist to it. He personally did the makeup for the lead singers, while his associates attended to other cast members. Because each singer's transformation required about half an hour, he would summon us to the makeup room in sequence, according to our onstage appearance. Baritones usually make entrances later than the other characters in most operas, so I was frequently last to occupy the chair. By this time the overture had begun, and there was a more relaxed attitude, as Elsen Associates prepared for the next makeup and wig change. Meanwhile, every gay man not onstage instinctively migrated to the room to hear Charles relate his most recent exploits to the assembled.

The subject matter rarely altered. Charles was intimately familiar with every gay bar and bathhouse in America, and his experiences were legendary. The stories usually involved bizarre, "over the edge" sex acts with multiple sex partners. At this stage of my life, I wasn't easily shocked, but some of his descriptions of the size and variety of objects used for penetration were beyond imagination.

This was circa 1981, still a few years before the Centers for Disease Control assigned a name to the epidemic that was silently but inexorably sweeping through the gay community. A time before the jocularity of these carefree tales took on a different tone. As the years passed, they became interspersed with dark jokes and nervous expressions about the possible repercussions of such promiscuity.

A few years later, at the dress rehearsal of a Baltimore production of *Rigoletto*, I took my place in front of the mirror. Dennis Bergevin, Elsen's business partner, stepped up to apply my makeup. I breezily asked him where his illustrious leader was. His eyes glazed a bit, and he told me Charles was too ill to come on the road. My heart skipped a beat. I pondered my response for a minute and then asked the unthinkable question, "Is it AIDS?"

In an environment that was usually boisterous to an extreme, you could have heard a pin drop.

"We don't know yet. We hope not," he said quickly.

But there was little confidence in his voice. The terrible reality had struck closer to home than any of us ever expected.

By the time I saw the Elsen team again a few months later, Charles had been diagnosed. He died of spinal meningitis the following year at age thirty-nine. He was the first in a long list of my colleagues who would fall to the disease. By the end of the decade, fully half of my gay friends and colleagues were gone. Then AIDS jumped the gap to heterosexuals. In a flash, the good times of untroubled, promiscuous sex were over.

Elsen Associates continued bravely after Charles's death and recently celebrated their thirtieth anniversary—a melancholy success story in the theatrical world.

◥ Under the Gun

Sitting in your hotel room the day of a performance, waiting to go to the theater, is an agonizing experience. It must be how soldiers feel before battle: the taste of metal in your mouth, the ants in your stomach. You're hungry, but you can't eat. You're sleepy, but you can't sleep. You feel like you've had enough caffeine to launch the Space Shuttle, and concentrating on anything for more than a few seconds is impossible. You want to crawl out of your skin. Your entire existence, and the future of your career, rests on how well you perform when you step out on that stage.

As I climbed the ladder of success and began taking on some of the most formidable roles in the baritone repertory, everything changed. For example, I started to believe my reviews—the great ones, at least, and there were plenty of those. I felt as if I was a demigod in the making, capable of soaring to the highest reaches of Mount Olympus. But gods at such lofty attitudes have a long way to fall, and any misstep can start the plunge.

I learned a cherished lesson during this period from soprano Carol Neblett, who advised, "Never read reviews."

She was right. If they're good, you're elated; if they're bad, you're despondent. A lousy review can make you doubt your existence. If you believe the good ones, you have to give the bad ones some credence as well. So why give some idiot that power over you?

As Deepak Chopra counsels, I learned "to be free of the good opinion of other people," especially if the *others* were critics. If I already had the gig and the check was in my hand before I stepped onstage, screw 'em if they didn't like me.

Thus, for the last half of my career I never read a single review. Instead, I had the publicity office of the individual opera companies send reviews to Louise, so she could dice and splice them for publicity purposes. It was a welcome relief to have that weight off my shoulders.

I stopped reading notices after receiving a disastrous review for *L'Amore dei Tre Rei* at New York City Opera, the same production I had premiered at the Kennedy Center the year before that brought me a mountain of accolades.

But it was fall in New York, and the tree pollen, or some such crap, was everywhere. I was hoarse. It was a hoarseness that prednisone would not touch. I was singing the show with bass Sam Ramey, which was fun, since we were often mistaken for each other in the halls of the State Theater, before he reached superstar status.

So there I was, on stage with Sam singing a duet, and my voice was just not working. It was torture! I went to my dressing room and hid after the performance. Beverly Sills, who had recently taken the mantle of artistic director from Julius Rudel, knocked on the door to congratulate me.

I said, "Beverly, you've got to be kidding! That was the worst performance I've ever sung here."

She responded to the effect of, "Well, it wasn't that bad," but I knew she was just trying to be nice. It turned out to be one of my last performances at NYCO.

So began my bouts with sudden, unexplained hoarseness.

The lifestyle of a singer is ripe for paranoia and hypochondria. If you think athletes have rituals, you haven't seen anything. The slightest inconsistency in The Voice on the day of a show can be worrisome. A bad night's sleep, exposure to dust or pollen, smoke, dry air, cold air—or any kind of air—spicy food, and a list of unimaginable things may bring on a tickle, which becomes a cough, which ... Ohhhhh, God!

Earlier in my career, I was not susceptible to such things. I remember being on a bus-and-truck tour of *The Barber of Seville*, standing backstage nonchalantly drinking a thick, chocolate milkshake just before going out to sing the "Largo," a tough piece under any circumstances. My colleagues were astounded.

Milk products are notorious for producing phlegm, but I was oblivious and unaffected. My voice always worked, and nothing short of cigarette smoke could irritate my throat.

In those days, smoking was permitted on airplanes, and my reaction to smoke was often so severe I had to fly in at least two days before the first rehearsal just to make sure I recovered.

As for singers' rituals, most begin theirs the week before a performance, especially opening night. It consists of a careful diet, sleep-producing atmospheres, and an adherence to whatever sexual routines one might have. By the way, singing isn't like boxing, where the principals sometimes abstain before the fight.

Remember the line from Rocky? "Women weaken legs." In show biz, the attitude toward sex is the more, the better, and there's a lot more of it going on behind the curtains than you'd ever imagine.

More than sex, however, sleep—lots of it—is a singer's best friend. To rephrase a great pianist's quote about a lack of practice, a bad night's sleep will show up at some point during the performance, and you as the singer will be the only one to notice. But after a series of bad nights, the audience will notice, too.

To get that vital, rejuvenating rest, singers will resort to just about anything, from exercise to meditation to drugs, to idiosyncratic sexual practices. Anything goes.

Where other musicians can be partiers during the run of a show, singers, though there are exceptions, tend to be loners, afraid that exposure to somebody with a lurking illness might give them a disastrous infection. A cold is a singer's only natural enemy, the single wildcard that singers fear most. After weeks of rehearsal and out-of-town expenses, a common cold that moves into the throat can kill your payday and the entire gig.

Several years into my career I became susceptible to colds and took extraordinary measures to avoid them. I took a vast array of drugs, both over-the-counter and prescription. In fact, it became so widely known that I carried cures in my little black bag I was dubbed with the nickname "Doc." Friends and colleagues were "referred" to me. It was not unusual to receive frantic calls or knocks on the door in the middle of the night with requests for help. My cold remedy was so often requested I eventually wrote it down, and by the time faxes and email became commonplace, I could zap it to anybody, anywhere in the world.

But once you have an infection, even a good remedy might not save the day. Singers become masters of tip-toeing around a part when they're in trouble. They learn which phrases to give away, how to pace themselves, and what notes will redeem them, like a tired fighter coasting for the first two minutes of a round only to bring it on in the last thirty seconds to steal it from his opponent.

The intense scrutiny of a singer's life is stressful, and perhaps this explains why they seem to have shorter life spans than many of their colleagues. Not surprising, organists and conductors seem to be the survivors of the business, frequently living to a ripe old age. With organists, it seems to have something to do with the constant exercise of both arms and legs. For conductors, it's all about the power…

The Conductor, *Il Primo Uomo*

"The conductor took unto himself more and more the direction of the performance ... By the end of the century the conductor was firmly established as the new "prima donna" in the world of music. Just as Handel had voiced the feelings of many of his 18th century colleagues when he inveighed against the liberties that singers took with their arias ... so Verdi, towards the end of that century, complained that the conductor had now replaced the singer as the composer's worst enemy."

—Music in the 19th Century, *Larousse Encyclopedia of Music*

While the conductor has always been a part of operatic performances in some capacity since the art form's origin, the emergence of the conductor as a dominant force in the rest of classical music did not occur until the beginning of the nineteenth century, with the larger and more complicated works of Beethoven and his contemporaries. As this growing artistic power melded with various administrative responsibilities, the conductor was forged into the most formidable entity in music, even overshadowing great soloists. This omnipotence is even apparent in the title "Maestro." Bestowed on most conductors, regardless of any true measure of their skills, it can be irksome to musicians confronted with an incompetent presiding over the podium.

"Beware! An orchestra is a savage beast. Never step before the monster unprepared, lest you be eaten alive."

This is a warning given to young conductors. It represents quite a different portrayal of the benign, formally clad musicians we are accustomed to seeing in the world's concert halls. Yet this warning has validity. In the highly ritualized domain of professional musicians, there is very little room for nonsense. These artists can smell bullshit a mile away, and unless you, as conductor, have the will to make your musical ideas prevail, they will tear you limb from limb with the same coolness a Mafia hit man might use to "whack" a victim.

Musicians can be stern and humorless when it comes to their craft. "It's not personal, it's just business," they'll say. No wonder conductors like the infamous Arturo Toscanini tended to have such severe, unyielding personalities. They run a wide gamut, and the ones who understand that more can be achieved with honey than vinegar usually get the best results.

It's difficult to describe the experience of standing before a large group of skilled musicians, bringing down the baton, and feeling them respond with a tidal wave of music. With a well-trained orchestra, the smallest gesture results in some organized response. It's like manipulating the strings of a massive musical marionette, only the result is something far more sublime. The exhilaration of that moment is almost unrivaled by anything else. It's the greatest power trip of all. It even challenges the intoxicating experience of standing onstage, hooking into that perfect high note, and feeling the sensation of thousands of people screaming "Bravo" wash over you from the darkness. No matter how loud you can sing, it doesn't approach the magnitude of sound you can generate with an orchestra of seventy-five players, or more.

I did some conducting in my early years, two-piano productions of operas and musicals and other small ensembles. But as my singing career blossomed, and I moved away from an instrumentalist's life, those experiences waned until after my retirement from the stage. My fascination with conducting and conductors, however, did not. With few exceptions my closest friends and colleagues were conductors. I didn't associate with stage directors for the most part and, with a few notable exceptions, the women I hung out with were little more than sex objects. So aside from the usual male-talk with the guys, most of my social and intellectual interactions were for, and about, music.

Artists in the ascending echelons of music live and breathe

their profession. It isn't the kind of world where you punch out at 5 p.m., leave your troubles on the doorstep, and then, martini in hand, tune in the daily tragedies on CNN. Well … maybe the martini part is okay.

An artist—especially a successful musical artist—is self-directed. Nobody watches over you, checking to see if your assignment is complete. You and you alone are responsible for your preparedness and proficiency. You either cut the mustard, or you don't. It's a twelve-hour-a-day job filled with private lessons in your specified discipline, lots of study, memorization, language coaching, or dance classes.

During my career, I learned, memorized, and performed more than forty roles in four different languages. As a conductor, later in life, I learned hundreds of orchestral works. The learning process never ceases. When a casual observer thinks you're daydreaming or experiencing some sort of manic episode while humming, drumming, or whistling, in reality you're studying and ruminating, repeating words and notes in your head for the thousandth time, until they become fluid, natural, and "unpracticed." To non-musicians, this can be disconcerting. But these quirky behaviors are commonplace among the craft, and they actually help us recognize one another.

I was passing through Haneda Airport in Tokyo, en route once again to Hong Kong, when I heard somebody whistling a strain from a Mendelssohn symphony—and whistling it well. I looked around and saw two Caucasians sitting in a food court.

I walked up to them and said, "Hi. Are you guys string or wind players?"

They laughed. It turned out they were string players touring Japan with an orchestra. There we were, previously strangers in an alien land, revealed to one another as members of a brotherhood by the whistling of a simple tune.

This kind of serendipitous collision of kindred spirits, amidst the great sea of humanity, can be magical, an unexpected home-coming miles from home. A melding, as indiscernible to those on the outside as the invisible signals that keep migrating birds together in a complex flight pattern. That chance encounter made me smile all the way to the South China Sea.

❧ *Andante Con Moto*

❧ Study, Study, Study!

It's difficult to explain how it feels to have dozens of roles cataloged in your brain, each ready at a moment's notice. Jumping from one opera to another is a schizophrenic experience. I could climb into the skin of a wretched court jester one day and adopt the elegant demeanor of a European aristocrat the next.

It takes a special kind of memory and a detailed preparation to do this. Though they've dimmed a bit over the years, even now fragments of these operas remain in my head. I can sit at a piano, play through the music and connect the dots, and within a couple of days it's all back, shiny and new. Having absorbed these roles, not to mention all of the other music I've learned over the decades, has created a barrier against loneliness. All I have to do is climb back into one of the characters and run the opera in my mind. Immediately I'm swept to another place, with as much reality as if I'd been zapped there by a transporter beam.

Learning new repertory is a never-ending process. In my late thirties, with forty-plus roles under my belt, I reached the point where I was ready to settle into my favorite eight or ten operas. I wanted to coast for a while and refine what I already knew. My goal was to amass a tidy nest egg, rest on my laurels, and wait for the next great opportunity. But offers I couldn't refuse came my way. One such contract was for Eugene Onegin, in Russian.

Accepting this was a difficult decision. My schedule had me bouncing around the country with no free time to learn something like this. But a chance to debut with Philadelphia Opera in a title role was just too good to pass up.

I thought of a *Fanciulla* I had done in Miami, many years before. During rehearsals, Placido Domingo flew back and forth from our rehearsals in Miami to the Met's production of *Chénier*. He struggled to keep the roles separated yet fresh in his mind. Like every singer, he wanted to accumulate as many paydays as possible while he still had the chops.

Remembering this, I signed the *Onegin* contract.

But how could I learn a completely unfamiliar language in such a short time? Lucky for me, my manager arranged for a renowned Russian-language coach at the Met named Cehanovsky. He was a lovely, elderly gentleman with enormous patience. We met a few times in a rehearsal room. He sat there with his eyes closed and spoke each line of the role, never referring to the score, while I recorded him. I took the tape home and mimicked his pronunciation and inflections. At the next meeting I repeated what I had learned, and he corrected me. Then I left town on a mad series of engagements, with only his taped voice for reference.

I arrived in the City of Brotherly Love on a frostbitten day in April. It was unseasonably cold. The cast was all eastern European except for me and tenor John Alexander in one of his last performances. The company reserved a hotel apartment for me in a building that had no central heating. The only heat sources were the oven and an air-conditioning/heating unit in the bedroom window, both of which I ran constantly. The cold was pervasive. Even running the heaters full-blast only provided as much relief as a lighted candle in Carlsbad Cavern.

My Tatiana was Teresa Zylis-Gara, a Polish soprano from the Met. We didn't hit it off from the very first rehearsal, and she made no effort to hide her disdain for me. Maybe it was my youth, or maybe it was just our lack of chemistry.

I overheard another cast member say that with me in the part, Zylis-Gara looked like Onegin's mother. I didn't think the contrast was that striking, especially from the stage. But whatever the reason, she didn't like me and there was nothing to be done. We had to sing opposite each other and learn to get along for two miserable weeks. I had no feelings about her one way or the other. I just wanted to escape the freezing cold of my room, sing the gig, get my check, and head toward the equator as soon as possible.

Speaking of freezing, Tchaikovsky wrote some magnificent ballets and orchestral music, but his operas leave me Siberian-cold. The tunes rarely take off, and the keys are often unflattering to The Voice. Only a few composers are true masters of vocal music, and most of them are Italian. Russian composers occasionally grab the thread of a great melody but just can't seem to weave it into an entire opera. And if they do, they give the great tunes to the orchestra—or the tenor. I'm not sure which is more annoying.

The day we staged the huge ballroom scene was the breaking point. Zylis-Gara and I started to waltz. Suddenly she stopped and began laughing.

She said, "Can you imagine? An Onegin who can't waltz!"

I was speechless. I thought she was stepping on my toes. But what the hell, this actually gave me a wonderful excuse to enlist the help of a particularly lovely ballerina from the corps de ballet. During some after-hours "rehearsal," we got a pretty nice pas de deux going, and I also learned a thing or two about the waltz. I think subconsciously my motivation might have had more to do with her warm apartment than improving my dance steps or getting laid.

Despite my tutoring, every time Zylis-Gara and I tried to dance, it was a mess. We were like two dancing bears, lumbering to different tunes. I zigged; she zagged. We lurched and bumped into everybody around us. It was like trying to push two positive ends of a magnet together. No matter how hard we tried, an invisible force thrust us apart. The director caught wind of this and made our waltz as short as possible, quickly paring us with other partners.

The performances were anticlimactic. Nobody got very good reviews, and the audiences were inscrutable. I was never happier to leave a city—except maybe Groningen.

❧ Riding the Crest

"One of the great achievements in the performance is the magnificent singing of baritone, Charles Long. What a treasure! His voice, flawlessly produced, is a clear ringing instrument of rich, beautiful power, capable of heroic passion and touching sympathy, both of which he uses devastatingly as the innocent Manfredo. Here is an artist of marvelous bearing who can be called ideal, one we should hear at every opportunity."
—Paul Hume, *The Washington Post*

"Charles Long was the 'Rigoletto' and he sang his heart out while breaking yours. His baritone was mature, secure, and heavy with beauty."
—*Detroit Free Press*

"Charles Long was perfection in the title role; I doubt if Tchaikovsky could have envisioned such a bold, clear voice in such an elegantly handsome frame."
—*Honolulu Star-Bulletin*

"Charles Long's 'Scarpia' is the most sadistic, violent and superb I have seen, other than the matchless characterization of Tito Gobbi. He is a stunning and growing artist."
—Paul Hume, *The Washington Post*

"Charles Long made an instant success in the title role. I predict a

spectacular career. He would seem to belong in the royal line of Tibbett, Thomas, Warren, Merrill, and Milnes."
—Charles Jahant, *Opera London*

Even if you're committed to avoiding them, reviews get back to you in news releases and publicity. And if the vast majority repeats the same thing, you start believing them. Likewise, if your friends and colleagues bestow upon you similar adulation, you're talking about some heady stuff.

This is good—and bad. If your identity is already synonymous with what you do, such input reinforces the fusion, making any future separation anxiety even more cataclysmic. The fact that so many believed I had been ordained to fulfill a remarkable destiny added to my extreme desire to attain that legacy. That, together with my earliest desires for fame and recognition, reinforced a neurotic, obsessive desire to succeed.

There's nothing as intoxicating and seductive as success. In a man's world, it is the primary commodity by which people judge you. Women can be treasured for their beauty, charm, and talent. But a man, no matter how gifted, is viewed as a failure without the trappings of financial, careered success. Success equals money, and money equals power. Not necessarily power over others but the power of freedom—the freedom of association and the free-dom of time. A person with money is rich. A person with time is wealthy. I wanted both. Life isn't fair, and affluence is the only way of reaping all the things life has to offer.

I knew this was my one chance to be successful. I had invested decades in the quest and had done it my way. I had lucked out. All my unusual skills came together in the odd discipline called opera. I may not have been cut out to do much in the real world, but I was unquestionably born to do this. I knew that without some unique form of expression at the core of my life, I would be in dire straits.

Not that I worried. I was singing my favorite roles all over the country. Working only eight months a year, I was earning a nice income, my father finally stopped asking me when I was going to get a real job, and it seemed I had made a mark for myself. I was a respected artist in a highbrow profession, and I was my own man. I was just moving into my best years, and I owed allegiance to no one.

My life was gliding along toward a nice crest when Penny and I decided to move to Los Angeles, partly to be closer to her family and partly because I had never liked New York. I was established enough that auditions were rarely necessary, and I'd already performed the majority of the roles I'd be doing for the rest of my career. I didn't need New York anymore. I'd paid my dues.

Thoughts of moving to the West Coast made me giddy. Images of living in a house, perpetually beautiful weather, and a "real life" danced like sugarplums in my head. But Penny was reluctant. She was still tied to the theatrical community in New York, hoping to land another Broadway musical. The discovery of some bodies dumped in an alley behind our building, however, gave our Exodus a new impetus. She agreed to go.

The day we packed the moving van she received a second callback for the show *Sunday in the Park with George.* But she sighed and just kept packing. If there was work in New York, there had to be more in L.A., right?

Right.

❧ Relationships: A Rocky Road

Maintaining a successful relationship is one of the ultimate challenges for people in show business. Relationships are complicated enough when you have a normal life. But when you include long periods of separation and the added temptations of rubbing shoulders—and a few other body parts—with highly attractive, charismatic people, the problems grow exponentially.

The magazines lining the counters of every grocery store in America exist almost exclusively by following the diets and sexual exploits of celebrities. Classical musicians and Broadway stars don't engender the same level of interest as Hollywood types, but they do share the same lifestyle, and the inner circles of their industries are ablaze with scandalous stories.

Many show biz relationships start via an illicit affair on the road. The infidelity rate is astonishing. A lot of humping goes on out there, and if the temptation toward extracurricular sexual activity is continual, by one or both partners, you may as well call the undertaker, because it's over. Passion, love, infidelity, and betrayal create a perpetual cycle. And so it goes. It's no surprise that few relationships born of infidelity succeed.

In order to do what they do, performers cultivate an open valve to their psyche. Emotions are close to the surface, and even the darkest corners of the id—which most people sublimate—are oiled daily with therapeutic glee.

Events and experiences become bigger than life in a rehearsal/performance environment. Performers mimic intimate relationships with strangers on a daily basis, so it's easy to believe these interactions are more meaningful than they really are. While struggling to suspend disbelief, as all actors must do, they often tend to create a fantasy world, in which they themselves are deluded.

When I initially moved to New York, I immediately started a relationship with a woman I had met in college and subsequently worked with in summer stock. We were living together, and because she was five years older, her need to bond, marry, and settle down was keen. Mine was not, but I appreciated the stability our relationship provided. We married within the year, and as we were both pursuing the same dream, working with the same teacher, and singing the same gigs, it was easy to stay focused on the relationship.

Opportunities, and my enormous musical curiosity, propelled me up the ladder at a faster rate, and eventually we found ourselves miles apart, both figuratively and literally. Even though some resentment surfaced as my star ascended, she seemed content to become a stage wife. I went on the road while she stayed in New York. Since money was tight in those days, we couldn't afford the plane fare for her to join me on a regular basis.

While on the road, I inevitably had offers of female companionship, and having a higher libido than most, I accepted. Once I strayed, it set off a chain reaction. Here I was, a young, attractive, virile man, full of testosterone, and ... well ... I started to make up for lost time. In fact, it would be fair to say that my sexual curiosity became another obsession. Eventually, and predictably, one indiscretion became serious.

We met during a *Rigoletto*—wouldn't you know—and a brief, intense affair followed. Being astute enough to realize that a single mother with two children would throw a monkey wrench into my career goals, I broke it off.

Then I went all out.

I was at the height of my powers, and I craved everything my new celebrity status could bring me. One time, I was juggling three different women in the same production. We all were staying in the same hotel. I bounded from room to room, like a satyr on crack. I could not slake what had become an insatiable thirst. I'd seduce one woman in the wings, diddle another under her costume in the dressing room, and pick up some stray quim in the catacombs under the stage during intermission—all as part of my noble quest to find the world's finest fellatrix.

It became obvious. The truth couldn't be avoided. Anybody who could carouse and feign intimacy with so many people was not meant for a committed relationship. The writing was on the wall, but my wife and I managed to maintain a good front and not speak of it. Yet it remained beneath the surface, and it radically altered our best-friend status. You can't be a friend to somebody who has proven himself untrustworthy. And certainly I had. The damage was done; it became apparent there was no going back. We limped along.

Two years passed, and I was scheduled to sing another *Rigoletto* with the same soprano who had derailed me in that previous production. I had every intention of being completely professional, as I think she did, but after the first rehearsal we knew we were in trouble. There we were, rehearsing these deeply emotional scenes, holding each other, singing together, phrasing together, smelling each other's pheromones, and next thing we knew ... well ... that was that.

We were both smitten once again, and about a year later my wife and I separated. I gave her the Manhattan apartment and went out on my own. The aforementioned soprano and I fell into an on again/off again affair, experiencing typical relationship problems, only magnified, because we were both traveling all the time. We planned trysts between each other's engagements, but this placed added stress on our already impossible schedules. We met on the road occasionally, but eventually the reality of each knowing that the other was still bed-hopping killed it.

Interestingly, once I actually became available, the thrill seemed to vanish for her, and an old boyfriend crept back into the picture. He was willing to act as a stage husband and part-time father to her kids. I exited stage center, never to look back. I had married too young, and fortune had saved me from jumping from the frying pan into the fire.

I met her one more time, however. We were both scheduled to sing at the Filene Center at Wolf Trap Farm Park, outside Washington, D.C., on tour with NYCO. I booked a room at my favorite hotel, The River Inn, just down the street from the Kennedy Center. Some sort of air-controllers strike or something was in progress, and there was not a room available anywhere without a reservation.

While checking in, I noticed that my former paramour was listed to be bumped to another hotel. So I left a note at the front desk inviting her to share my room when she arrived. We hadn't spoken in a long time, and meanwhile I had become involved with a sex kitten who lived in Anchorage, Alaska—a long way off. We had just enjoyed a romantic rendezvous in London, and I really thought there might be something there. She had even invited me to come live with her in Alaska, and though that was more of a commitment than I was comfortable with at that point, I still didn't want to fuck it up.

Along with my room-to-share invitation, I left a message for Madame X that, should she accept this mission, she was not to answer the phone in my room. I didn't want any trouble on the remote chance that Miss Alaska might track me down to this hotel and try to call. Miss Alaska was in love, motivated, and very resourceful.

I left for rehearsal. When I returned, I asked at the desk if Madame X had arrived. They informed me that she had checked into my room. So I went upstairs to find her in all her splendor. Although eerie, it was just enough like old times to be exciting. We tiptoed around each other for the next few hours, but eventually, even though there were two beds, we ended up in the same one. Then she told me the phone had rung while I was gone and, thinking it might be one of her children, she picked it up and said hello.

Oh no! Was this the Universe kicking the shit out of me, or what?

She said a woman's voice asked her who she was, so she abruptly hung up. Too late! I knew the damage was done. I called Miss Alaska to explain the overbooking situation, but she wasn't having any of it.

A few weeks later I even flew to Alaska to try to appease her. It was a nice trip, but she was guarded. The trust had been broken. I'd managed to shoot myself in the foot, again. I'd met a hot, independent woman who only wanted to please me and offered to share her home with me, but I cast it aside for a trip to the moon with an old flame whom I didn't even like. What in the fuck was the matter with me?

I resumed my wandering and sampling. Sometimes I found it exciting, but more often it was unsatisfying, repetitive, and meaningless. To a man with a supercharged sex drive, however, quantity often trumps quality. On the other hand, I found being constantly on the prowl tiring and distracting. Certainly, it was not good for my career. I needed to find something more stable.

Then I met Penny, a foxy, eccentric colleague at City Opera. We had known each other casually for a couple of years. We often caught each other's eye while passing in the hall or flirting in rehearsal. But I was married at that time and had adopted a perverse honor system. When I was in New York and had access to my wife, I never cheated, but when I was on the road, the sky was the limit.

Penny and I had never been out of town together, so though we were attracted to each other, nothing ever happened. Then, by coincidence or synchronicity, we met outside the Lincoln Center Library the day I signed my divorce papers. I was a free man. I asked her to brunch. By that evening we were in the sack, and that was that.

We'd both been around the block, so we were feeling ready to settle down a bit. We shared much in common, and neither of us was interested in marriage, so we took our time. Within the next year we were sharing an apartment in upper Manhattan, commencing a relationship that has lasted—including one long hiatus—nearly three decades.

I had learned much from my first marriage, and with a newly acquired affluence, I spent the bucks to make sure we weren't apart more than two weeks. Even if it was for only one day, we would rendezvous somewhere.

Two such meetings stand out in my mind. The first was after I had finished another *Eugene Onegin* in Honolulu and was on my way to Columbus to do Enrico in *Lucia di Lammermoor*. Penny was in upstate New York playing Aldonza in *Man of La Mancha*. Because we'd been apart for a few weeks, I took a detour so we could be together for twenty-four hours. We spent most of it in bed.

It was freezing outside, and my blood was really thin from three weeks in Hawaii. We laughed, loved, played, and danced. But during the latter, I landed poorly, my ankle snapped, and I tore a ligament. It quickly blew up to the size of a football, and I could barely walk.

I had to be in rehearsal for a part I'd never performed in less than twelve hours. I wrapped the ankle and hobbled off to the airport to catch my flight. I managed to schlep all my luggage, make my connections, and get to Columbus in the nick of time.

The damage was severe, however. I elevated my foot and iced as much as possible during rehearsal, but two weeks later there was little improvement, so I literally limped through the performances. It didn't go unnoticed. One reviewer called it "an interesting character choice," and I continued to have trouble with the ankle for the next three months. But it had been worth it. Such detours were an investment in a valuable commodity in the changing world, and I was determined to do it right this time.

The next situation required special fortitude.

Penny and I were living in Los Angles. We'd rented a quaint

duplex in the Fairfax area of the city. We had a dog, family, friends, and a semblance of normalcy. I had my career, she had hers, and life was comfortable. For a thrill-seeker, however, comfort can be dangerous.

I was in New Orleans doing *Carmen* with one of the most beautiful mezzos in the business—a South American heartbreaker. The first time I saw her at NYCO, I thought I would stop breathing. She was the epitome of my type: dark-skinned, exotic, bedroom eyes, and a figure that stopped traffic. She had a sultry Latin gait, like a silk scarf in a light breeze.

Though we knew each other, we had never worked together. And wouldn't luck have it, we hit it off famously. Our interactions followed a predictable pattern. We flirted in rehearsal, ate meals together, and took evening walks through the French Quarter, which is romantic even if you're alone.

She had a part-time boyfriend in New York, and I had been very open about my relationship, but we both knew where this was headed. The attraction was so intense I was powerless to stop it.

I called Penny one night and when she asked how I liked working with Miss South America, I replied, "Pen, she's great. And if she comes knocking on my door in the middle of the night, I won't be able to say no."

Penny grabbed the next flight out of LAX, and I knew I had passed an enormous hurdle. But to say I didn't feel a little bit cheated or have fantasies about this missed opportunity would be a lie. Addiction is addiction, and no drug does it for me like women. I was able to forestall the inevitable, but I was who I was, and even splinters buried deep eventually work their way out.

Manon Lescaut in Tulsa

A short time after I signed with Louise, she arranged an audition with Tulsa Opera. Normally this would have been a simple afternoon's work, because every major opera company periodically holds auditions in New York. But I had missed Tulsa when they were in town—or they missed me, I don't remember which—and Louise didn't want them to book the season before hearing me. So the deal was this: They would hold off on casting if I would fly to Oklahoma at my own expense to audition.

I balked at this, but Louise had a hunch, and I wanted to show her I had faith in her instincts. So, I booked a round-trip ticket—a huge financial stretch at the time—and brushed up on my standard audition pieces.

It was a four-hour flight, so I opted to go the day before. Louise made the hotel arrangements through the opera company, and off I went.

When I arrived in Tulsa, I took a cab from the airport to the address I'd been given. It was a motel in a suburban part of town. I was tired and hungry, and all I wanted was a meal and a good night's sleep. Unfortunately, there were no restaurants within view. After querying the office clerk, I discovered that the closest place was a considerable distance. He suggested I take a cab. Determined not to spend a dime more than necessary, I set out on foot and found a small restaurant, ordered some take-out, and hiked back to my room.

By now it was early evening, and the opera company hadn't contacted me. No welcome note, no "How to Get around Town" pamphlet, no "see you later" message. Nothing. I would've welcomed a "Go to Hell" note. Anything. I started wondering if I'd made a mistake. Perhaps I had the wrong date? Had I come all the way to Tulsa to sing when nobody knew or cared? It was unsettling.

I called the number Louise had given me for the opera office. It was after hours. A voice on an answering machine instructed me to leave a message. I said Charles Long had arrived in town for his audition and would see Mr. Purrington, the director of the company, at the appointed time the next day. I had no idea where, of course, but there seemed no point in sharing this with a disembodied voice.

I tossed and turned for hours, wishing I had something to help me sleep. Sensations of weird crawled around me. I felt like I was living in a "Twilight Zone" episode. Good things rarely happened to people in the Twilight Zone, and in typical horror-genre style, they always had warning signals of impending doom but chose to ignore them. Finally, I fell into a fitful unconsciousness.

Morning came early. I pulled myself out of bed and checked the mirror to assure myself I that hadn't turned into a werewolf during the night. Then I hiked about a mile, until I found a small diner serving breakfast. I ate quickly and headed back to the motel.

Still no messages.

I was starting to freak. The audition was only a few hours away, and I hadn't been contacted by anybody. I called the office again, and a woman with a soft Oklahoma drawl answered the phone. I told her I had an audition with Mr. Purrington, and I didn't know where to go or how to get there. She put me on hold for a long time, and when she came back, she said, "Well, Honey, Mr. Purrin'ton's not here, and I don't know anythin' about an audition, but here's the address. You tell any cab driver and he'll know where to go."

Clunk.

This was getting stranger by the minute. What should I do? There was no good reason to call Louise. There was nothing she could do from New York. So, I dressed, packed my briefcase, called a cab, and set off.

Twenty minutes later, the cab pulled up in front of a flat and unremarkable building. Just like everything else in Tulsa. I paid the cabbie and went inside. There was no reception desk, just a maze of fluorescent-lit corridors with offices lining both sides. I wandered the halls, looking for signs of life, popping my head into one after the other, asking for Mr. Purrington.

"I'm here for an audition," I smiled.

I was greeted with blank stares. Some of the offices didn't even seem to belong to the opera company, nobody knew who this guy was, and certainly nobody knew anything about an audition. After checking nearly every office in the building, I finally accosted a nice woman who offered me a seat and said she'd find somebody who could help me.

Time passed.

Fifteen minutes before I was due to sing, a guy walked up and introduced himself by his first name, which I immediately forgot, and then escorted me to a rehearsal room.

"Mr. Purrington should be along any minute," he explained.

I was alone, so I figured I'd use the occasion to vocalize. I hadn't sung since the morning before, and after a long flight with a lot of smokers on board, I hoped The Voice was going to work. I tried a few scales and figured I was at about 85 percent, which under the circumstances wasn't bad. I'd probably sing an aria or two and then be on my way. No big deal.

I waited.

No one arrived. I sang a few more scales.

Finally, two people walked in. There were no introductions, but I suspected one of them was Ed Purrington and the other a pianist, since he asked if I had any music. The man I assumed to be Purrington regarded me with an expression someone might make if they discovered a piece of chewing gum on the sole of their shoe. He said something about "beginning" and seated himself in a chair at the other end of the room. I took out my music, gave it the pianist, and began to sing.

When I finished, the Purrington suspect asked if I had brought anything else. I rattled off a list of arias, and he picked one. I sang.

Then he asked for another. I sang again.

He mused for a moment and asked for another. I sang for the fourth time. My voice was starting to get tired. I mean, these were all big, blockbuster pieces. No fluff. I had started singing with less than a full arsenal, so I was starting to run out of ammo, and I desperately needed a drink of water.

Incredulously, when I finished the fourth aria, before I could even take a breath, the man asked if I had any else. I thought of strangling him with a nearby electrical cord, but instead I asked where the water fountain was. Looking almost annoyed that I'd forced a break in the action, he gave me impatient directions. I took a long drink and with a sigh, walked back to the room, girding myself for the next onslaught.

The last piece is the only one I remember singing. It was the Toreador Song from *Carmen*, and it was a struggle. I was shot.

If he asks for anything else, I thought, *I'll have to bludgeon both of them with my briefcase and hide the bodies in the grand piano. In this place, nobody would discover them for weeks.*

But mercifully, without any emotion at all, he said "Thank you" and unceremoniously started to leave. Before he could get away, I quickly asked if I could get a ride back to the motel. Almost absent mindedly, he said, "Well … I guess that could be arranged."

I remember getting a ride to the motel, but how I got to airport I have no recollection. I do remember the harsh mumblings I made the whole way back to New York.

Man, if I don't get something from this, there's no justice in the world!

Did you know there's no justice in the world?

Months passed, and I never heard a word. The months became years. Then fully ten years after that dreadful day, Tulsa offered me a contract for Manon Lescaut.

About fucking time!

It turned out that Ermanno Mauro was the tenor and Anton Coppola the conductor—really good signs. The soprano was some Brit I'd never heard of, but I figured she must be damn good to have been brought all the way across several time zones and put at the top of such a strong cast.

I had done *Manon Lescaut* with Carol Neblett in Seattle, when she debuted the role. She was a splendid Manon and far and away my favorite Minnie in *Fanciulla*. Carol was always fun to work with. She was attractive, bright, and extremely well prepared. Because we were the same size and had that blonde, blue-eyed, all-American, apple-pie look, sometimes people mistook us for brother and sister. This made the task of playing siblings in *Manon Lescaut* all that much easier.

Anyway, whoever the British gal was, she had some pretty impressive shoes to fill in this part, as far as I was concerned.

I arrived for the first musical run-through, and the Brit, whose name I honestly don't remember, was very nice. But, like so many European singers with whom I had worked before, she was still on her score at the first rehearsal—and the second, and the third. This led me to conclude she hadn't done the role before, and I wondered why she'd been hired. She had no special talent to recommend her for the part, and there were so many good American sopranos.

British Commonwealth countries had, at that time, a quota system for performing artists. Companies were required to fill a large percentage of available roles with Commonwealth singers. Foreigners could not be imported to do parts as long as there was a performer in the Commonwealth who could sing the role.

America's doors, in contrast, were wide open. British, Canadian, Australian, or other singers of the Commonwealth were consistently hired to sing here, putting Americans out of jobs. The lack of reciprocity galled me. So, whenever I worked with Canadians—or Brits, especially—I expected them to be remarkable. If they weren't, I was not overly friendly.

When we started the staging rehearsals, our Manon was still on the score most of the time and having difficulty with everything. She dropped cues and constantly stood in the wrong place on the set.

One day, near the end of rehearsals, we were blocking the trio in the second act. Each time we tried to do the scene, Manon would stop singing and wander around center stage looking bewildered. It was the only time I ever recall Anton Coppola losing it. He stopped the rehearsal and said, "Ermanno, Charles, go home. You shouldn't have to go through this."

Then he looked sternly at Manon and said, "You and I will stay here until you learn this. Get your score." And with that, Coppola started the trio again, as Ermanno and I tiptoed out.

We rarely saw Purrington during rehearsals, which was surprising, considering the trouble the soprano was having. But during production week he started making cameo appearances and engaging the cast in small talk. Though I still had a bit of resentment about that audition ten years before, in the spirit of camaraderie, I was willing to let bygones be bygones.

Purrington seemed amiable enough. Maybe I had caught him on a bad day. But, hey, there's no way it could have been worse than mine. Still, you never know. So I let it go and put my best foot forward. I knew that Ermanno and "Queen Elizabeth" both had contracts for future seasons, so I thought if I played my cards right, perhaps I would, too.

We opened, and though she had some shaky moments, Manon got through the show. I think there was some talk of giving her a prompter—as they often do in Europe—but Coppola vetoed it.

We did three performances, with a week between the second and third. I had intended to return to L.A. between shows and save myself the cost of living expenses, which were considerable in this oil rich town. So, after the second performance, I called, as a courtesy, to inform the staff that I'd be leaving. Actually, there's a stipulation in AGMA contracts requiring artists to get "permission" to leave town, but nobody pays much attention to it.

As I was packing, the phone rang. It was Ed Purrington.

"I heard you're planning to leave town," he said.

"Yes. There's no reason to stick around here and pay another week of hotel bills. I'm going back to L.A. After all, I've got a life."

"Oh ... well ... you see, there's a fundraiser on Thursday, and it's traditional for the soloists to attend and interact with the Board."

"Really? Tradition, huh? I sure don't see anything about tradition in my contract," I replied.

"I'm sure you can understand how important fundraising is. We want to make sure that we have enough money for future seasons. Therefore participation in these events is in everybody's best interest. Both your colleagues will be there," he assured me.

"Excuse me, Ed, but my colleagues both have contracts for future seasons—I don't," I countered.

He was clearly surprised by my knowledge of this. There was dead air on the phone. Finally, I said, "Hello?"

"Your contract says you must stay in town unless given permission to leave," he replied firmly.

Oops! That was the wrong thing to say to me, so I shot from the hip.

"That may be, Ed, but my contract says nothing about attending a fundraiser and schmoozing the Board of Directors. So if I were to stay, I wouldn't do your fundraiser unless I had a contract in my hand, just like Ermanno and Eliza Doolittle."

Silence.

I went on, "Now if I had a contract, then I'd agree that it would be in our best interest. But it took me ten years to get here, and I'm not giving anything away for free. Do you want to talk about a future contract?"

He hemmed and hawed. He had no idea how to counter this. Finally, with a cold voice he said, "I can't do that."

"Well, then I can't stay. Enjoy your fundraiser. I'll see you in a week."

I hung up. Purrington had jerked me around once. I wasn't going to give him a chance to do it again. I checked out and flew back to L.A.

I returned a week later to sing the last performance.

It's customary for the director to come by the dressing rooms after the last show and thank the artists. Ed didn't show up at mine, so I figured my first impression of him had been pretty accurate.

I left Tulsa with the knowledge that I'd never be asked back while Purrington was in charge, departing yet another company to which I'd been blacklisted. But I was satisfied I'd done the right thing. If you let people fuck with you, they will. It's just human nature.

🖎 Los Angeles

Life was pretty blissful during those few years in L.A. I was successful, in love, living in a beautiful climate, and all my wishes seemed to be coming true. Now, however, as I look back, I'm reminded of a warning whispered to conquering Roman heroes, as their chariots carried them through the streets of Rome: "All glory is fleeting."

I had always loved L.A. It's nothing like New York. It's sunny, warm, beautiful, laid-back and outdoorsy—a lifestyle that suits me perfectly. Also, instead of taking buses or subways, people drive. I like driving, and I like having my own space when I travel. I've never liked public transportation. I like to decide when, where, and how I rub elbows with the proletariat. I've driven to Las

Vegas and endured five hours in the scorching heat rather than take a one-hour flight, just so I wouldn't have to deal with people. My misanthropic nature mellows in the vastness of the Southwest.

I sold the car I had in New York and paid cash for a beautiful, racing-green MGB convertible. I was in Seventh Heaven: palm trees, miles of beach, mountains and, of course, smog. You can see it best from a plane or the heights of the San Gabriel Mountains; it's not as obvious while you're in the thick of it. Nonetheless, it's there. Looming. Insidiously doing its thing.

Penny tried to break into the film and TV industry, and I did my usual routine. Except for an enhanced lifestyle, our existence remained much the same. When I wanted it, there was a sense of family and activities. I always knew I wasn't cut out to be a father. I never had a desire to take on that responsibility. But as an uncle, I was stellar. Penny had a niece and three nephews, and I could borrow them whenever I wanted. At the end of the day, however, I knew I could return them to their parents. It was the best of all worlds.

It was at one of these family events in Simi Valley when the first signs appeared. About ten of us were playing touch football and, while I was running, I suddenly realized I was struggling for breath. It wasn't that I was winded or tired; I just couldn't pull enough air into my lungs. It was as though I'd inhaled something that was obstructing my airway.

Struggling for air is a panicky sensation. I'd never felt anything like it. I was startled, but I pushed myself through the difficulty, thinking it was some temporary aberration or a reaction to something in the grass.

I quickly put it out of my mind, since my health had always been perfect. Then, a few weeks later, while exerting myself, the same thing happened again. This time I commented on it, and a nephew who'd been struggling with it since childhood said, "It sounds like asthma."

What? At my age? How could that be?

A much bigger worry: I also noticed that when my breathing became labored, my voice became shredded and airy. It had no resonance. Obviously, whatever was causing my bronchial tubes to close was also affecting my trachea, larynx, and vocal cords. My respiration became noticeably shorter, and singing required more frequent, exaggerated breaths. Worse, my lungs misinterpreted the hyperventilation as exertion, which can spark an asthma attack.

I began noticing breaks in my voice during the next few performances. At first, they were small. Then, there were larger slips in places where The Voice had previously held without question. The length of my phrases became diminished, and when I had to inhale quickly, I couldn't take a full breath. Little things that in a normal person's life would have been mildly inconvenient became major ordeals.

I started having bouts of unexplained hoarseness. It felt like phlegm on my cords, except no amount of throat-clearing could dislodge it. Since it even occurred between engagements, when I was resting my voice, clearly it wasn't related to my singing.

I started seeing a long list of MDs: allergists; ear, nose and throat specialists; internists, and pulmonologists. They provided more questions than answers. None of them agreed on anything, except that I probably had a case of adult onset asthma. This was rare, but it explained the symptoms, except the persistent hoarseness. There were no nodules or any underlying pathology.

Why was I hoarse?

It was a mystery—an enigma that had emerged as a clear and present danger to my career. The more money I spent on doctors, the less I learned, except that medical professionals had little knowledge about the causes and etiology of asthma.

Michael Crichton, in his book *Travels*, talks about medical misadventures and his former profession's lack of connection with patients. More than anything, it convinced him after four years of medical school he didn't want to be a doctor.

I experienced this firsthand. With career-threatening symptoms, I went to doctor after doctor and received the same, apathetic mantra time and again. They gave me diagnoses ranging from asthma to tumor and from bronchial perforation to stridor, replete with a stack of prescriptions for the same prophylactic remedies that hadn't worked before. I was beside myself. Science had put men on the moon, cured terrible diseases, created artificial hearts, and transplanted organs from one person to another, yet they couldn't diagnose and treat my seemingly simple affliction.

With no alternatives, I forged ahead, trying to keep a daily diary of my symptoms, so that I might be able to predict my attacks. One day I would be perfectly fine, and the next I was unable to phonate at all. Other days, out of the blue, I was gasping for breath like a fish out of water.

Galvani and Cincy and Sills, Oh My!

Despite my vocal inconsistencies, I sang some of my finest performances during this period, including three memorable productions at Cincinnati Opera with Artistic Director Jim de Blasis and Maestro Anton Coppola: Verdi's *Attila* and *Il Trovatore* and Leoncallo's *Zaza*.

Cincinnati Opera mounted interesting works with entertaining casts of characters—on and off the stage—and Jim was a director of some note. Inventive and extremely efficient, he had helmed both the Pittsburgh and Cincinnati operas for a number of years. He was also a loyal friend.

Successful productions with congenial casts usually don't lend themselves to juicy narratives. Without drama or conflict, such collaborations often prove unmemorable. This was the predictable situation in Cincy, because Jim only hired friends and those he liked personally. He was very forthright about this practice and made no apologies. Temperamental singers were quickly dispatched and, as a result, Cincinnati Opera became a tight family of serious artists dedicated to one task: making Jim de Blasis happy. The results spoke for themselves.

Anton Coppola only stood about five-foot-three but with the personality of a Goliath. He was a member of the renowned Francis Ford Coppola family and displayed similar creative genius. Singing Italian opera with Coppola and his vast musical knowledge was always a treat. He rarely used a score in rehearsal, as every word and note was ingrained in him from decades of experience.

Attila featured Puerto Rican basso Justino Diaz. Gus, as he was called, was charming, roguish, debonair, and enormously talented. He could drink you under the table, smoke a pack of cigarettes, stay up all night carousing, and still sing like a god the next day. Remember the villain Zolo in the film *Romancing the Stone*? Well, he and Gus could have been twins.

Gus and I had done *Attila* together before at NYCO. The conductor was Sergiu Comissiona, a well-respected and skilled symphonic conductor. But while Comissiona was well-liked by the orchestra, his knowledge of voices and the musical characterization of the drama left a great deal to be desired.

Once, Gus and I were rehearsing a big duet and having fun blasting away at each other. It felt a lot like a vocal gun fight. But just when we were really getting into it, Comissiona stopped and began a confusing dissertation about the overlapping of the voices and his desire that we imitate two bassoons. At first, we thought he was joking. Then we realized the guy was serious. Neither Gus nor I were subtle singers—neither is Verdi's music.

I, being the undiplomatic, arrogant loudmouth I was, responded.

"Excuse me, but if you want this to sound like two bassoons, you should hire two bassoons. I used to play the bassoon, and this is too high in our voices to sing that lightly. Nor does it fit the drama of the scene. Do you have any idea what the characters are saying to each other?"

Of course he didn't, nor did he give a damn. He was a symphony conductor, and he brought that mindset to the theater. Just because he *could* conduct an opera didn't mean he *should*.

Jumping back to Cincinnati…

Also in the *Attila* cast was Marisa Galvani. I hadn't seen Marisa for years. The last time was when she sang *Maria Stuarda*—one of Donizetti's "Queen Operas"—at NYCO. Beverly Sills, the reigning house diva at the time, was slated to do Maria to Galvani's Elizabetta.

Galvani had a huge following in New York. She had a husky, Callas-like timbre, enough volume to peel paint, and a range to kill for. She could sing like a mezzo on the bottom and slam-out the top with the best dramatic coloratura. She was also an attractive woman *and* she could act—a triple threat. I have to give credit to Sills for giving somebody with Galvani's talent such an opportunity. But perhaps she had no power to stop it. I certainly know she lived to regret it.

Rehearsals with the two women were pretty civilized. Both frequently sang out but never enough to reveal any weakness.

Opening night had the same thrill as a Super Fight in Las Vegas. The house was packed with fans from each camp, and ovations bounced back and forth all night, as each diva had her moments.

They reached the famous court scene, where both women share the stage and duke it out. It culminates with a huge ensemble and a chance for the divas to take an interpolated high note. Galvani had marked this moment throughout rehearsal, like a fighter holding back in sparring sessions, not wanting to reveal the magic punch. But now she was ready for the kill.

Galvani stood upstage of Sills, as both sopranos went for the final note. But Galvani's was bigger—a lot bigger. Then she started a slow walk, right past Sills, to the edge of the proscenium. Sills held the note as long as she could, but Galvani held it longer. The curtain came down and the audience went mad. This was the way singers used to duel in the day of Donizetti, but in modern times, upstaging a reigning diva on her own turf was considered blasphemy.

The performances went on, and Galvani repeated the same event every night. She received critical acclaim, and her fan base swelled. But after the show closed, she was only to return to NYCO to sing second casts during Sills's tenure.

But here she was in Cincinnati, in typically great form, singing *Attila* with Enrico Di Giuseppe, Justino Diaz, and yours truly. Screamers all. Wonderful colleagues from a bygone era, singing opera the way it was meant to be sung.

🖎 *The Pearl Fishers* in Milwaukee

The last new role I learned was Zurga in Bizet's *The Pearl Fishers*. It was a good cast and the last time I worked with Cynthia Auerbach, a chain-smoking stage director with a personality like battery acid. I had first met Cynthia many years before in a production of *La Bohème*. She was one of the few stage directors I actually liked. She was highly intelligent, open to everybody's ideas, and willing to experiment.

Throughout my career, when there was a sticky place in the blocking, I would tell the director to leave it alone and let me dream about it. Literally. I would think about the scene right before sleep. I'd dream, and upon waking, the solution was clear. Many directors didn't like this at all. Cynthia got a kick out of it, because if it was a good idea she'd incorporate it into the production and in all future productions. It was win–win for everybody.

As the years went on, however, Cynthia's verve and good

nature were replaced with a hostile cynicism. Her low-pitched, New York accent became husky to the point of alarm, and her rail-thin body was frequently wracked with the most terrible cough. Her wit and good humor vanished, and by the time I saw her in Milwaukee, she looked like a walking cadaver—a real-life Mimi.

Regardless, she showed up at rehearsal every day and did her job. But it was all business. She resisted any input and glared at everybody, as she lit one cigarette after another. She couldn't stop smoking. We all understood. Cynthia was dying.

The tragedy surrounding these events set the mood for the production. And it was a dark one. I was between bouts of hoarseness, and my voice was in splendid shape, but I didn't like the opera, and all my colleagues seemed to be struggling with personal issues. It was winter in Milwaukee and an all-around upsetting gig.

The stage—or maybe it was the lighting—was constructed in such a way that it was easy to see the audience, which I've always found disconcerting. The thing I like about big theaters is the distance between me and the audience. The orchestra pit creates a buffer zone. They, the audience, are sitting in the darkness, while I am being worshipped in the light. Kind of like church, except without a sermon. And much better music.

Here, I could see the faces, though mostly I just saw blank stares. They had purchased expensive tickets and sat there obediently in a slack-jawed trance. At one point, while I was listening to the tenor sing a long section leading into our duet, I thought, *We're singing an opera with the most arcane plot, in French, with no subtitles. What are you people doing here? I'm not enjoying it—and I'm singing it!*

Much of the music was uncompelling, certainly not the ilk of *Carmen*, Bizet's masterpiece, and yet these people had come out on a freezing night to witness this spectacle. I was baffled. Something was happening. My unwavering love for the art form was faltering. What was this about?

In the last scene of the opera, my character is killed by a spear-thrust. In rehearsal, the supernumerary who was to stab me had been so tenuous that it was hard to fake the sensation of a fatal wound. So I encourage him to be a bit more forceful with his thrust. As the run went on, he became emboldened, and by the last performance, he hit me so hard he actually fractured my rib. I felt it snap like a rubber band and fell to the stage in agony. The scene played beautifully, however. A cracked rib was a small price to pay for such a real theatrical moment.

I left for Miami the next morning for a production of *Pagliacci*, soothing a throbbing chest and a growing cynicism about my profession. I never saw Cynthia Auerbach again. She died May 16, 1987, after a battle with lung cancer. She was forty-four years old

✒ *Pagliacci* in Beautiful Miami

I love Florida, and it was nice to be there after my bleak experience in Milwaukee. The sun felt good, and the air was balmy. I rented a car at the airport and drove to an apartment near Coconut Grove.

The last time I'd been to Miami, I saw Muhammad Ali fight a five-round exhibition. I was sitting just behind ringside in a small arena, watching an uninteresting middleweight bout, when I sensed a huge "light" coming from my left. No doors to the outside had opened, no spotlights were shining, yet there was this undeniable illumination originating at the edge of my peripheral vision. All heads in the arena turned in unison, as Ali, surrounded by his entourage, glided down the aisle.

I've always been skeptical about auras, mystics, and all that crap, but Ali projected a tangible presence as he walked by, and everybody in the arena felt it. Once he entered his dressing room, the sensation and illumination vanished.

A few preliminary fights took place before Ali appeared again. This time the glow was not of the same intensity, but it was still there. He fought a dismal five rounds, hardly throwing a punch, doing his famous "rope-a-dope" routine. But the crowd loved it, and I was so caught up in the essence of this man that I wasn't able to think of anything else.

But this trip to Miami didn't include any boxing. It was all business: a performance of Cav/Pag, a cast of hundreds, and my fractured rib. Rehearsals were pleasant, and I was in great company with Ermanno Mauro and Diana Soviero. I even managed to keep the pain under control, but on the night of the dress rehearsal, in the fight scene with Diana, my rib popped again. Moving, singing, breathing—anything—became excruciating. The company arranged for a doctor to shoot my ribs full of Lidocaine before the show.

Despite all this, the performances were satisfying, and I even got a chance to see my old friend Keith Baker, who was running a theater in West Palm Beach. We hadn't seen each other since we shared a loft in Soho several years earlier. We reminisced about the time we had gotten wasted on hash brownies and bemoaned our lives. We were broke at the time, divorced, and contemplating another line of work. Then, out of a stoned stupor, Keith said something that has always stayed with me.

"No matter how bad things get," he mused, "there's always a little voice in the back of your mind that says, 'You're an actor; you can use this!'"

And *I Puritani* at NYCO

My final experience at City Opera was a production of *I Puritani*, an opera that had never thrilled me. But since I was being offered the premiere, it was tough to refuse. My hoarseness once again was in remission, and I actually looked forward to a little New York exposure and seeing some of my old friends.

Rehearsals started off badly. The conductor, whose name I can't recall, was a frustrated singer who was driving everybody crazy. We'd sing a line of recitative, and he'd stop. Then he'd sing it for us. I couldn't tell the difference, but we'd repeat it again, imitating him as closely as possible. This happened with nearly every line in the opera, with each member of the cast, for days.

Needless to say, this kind of shit didn't go over very well with me. I was the guy hired to sing the part and interpret the lines, not him. If I'd wanted a coach, I would have hired one. In short, this clown was going to have to get off my case, or we were going to crack heads real soon.

So, I took preemptive action by taking him aside and explaining the situation. Rehearsal periods at NYCO were short, and his nit-picking about every fucking line wasn't helping matters. I suggested—in the nicest possible way, of course—that he should stop dicking around, do his job, and let me do mine.

I must have been persuasive, because he never stopped rehearsal again.

When I had arrived in New York, summer was in full swing. But now the blush of an early autumn adorned the trees, and a new set of allergens began to fill the air. It was the same setting I'd experienced for *L'Amore Dei Tre Rei* a few years before, and despite a dedicated regime of antihistamines and careful singing, I was fighting hoarseness by the end of the second week.

Damn!

I saw an ear, nose, and throat doctor and got a prescription for a large dose of prednisone. But I had a dry hoarseness that didn't respond well to medication. So, I laid back in rehearsal and hoped it would clear. I notified the office that I was struggling with allergies but expressed my belief that I'd be fine for the opening.

The next day a young baritone, whom I knew slightly, strode into the rehearsal and took a seat at the front. It was easy to guess he was my cover. Here he was, licking his chops, as I had done in the same room while watching Bill Chapman a decade before. The tide always turns, and everything has a cycle. I'd made the transition from hunter to hunted.

I tried to sing a bit, but The Voice wasn't cooperating. Then I thought maybe I'd muscle it in, but when I went for a high note it cracked. I was mortified. Nothing like that had ever happened to me. My cover bowed his head and left. That was the last straw. I stopped the rehearsal and said to the conductor, "My voice is shot. It's not getting better. I have to cancel."

He looked like he'd been hit by a lightning bolt and implored me to try again the next day. I assured him it would make no difference. I thanked him and my colleagues and left the rehearsal room, never to return to the New York State Theater again.

I called Beverly and gave her my apologies. I left New York with my tail between my legs, knowing an era had ended.

~ *Più Grave*

~ The Glory of Victory, the Agony of Defeat

To-morrow, and to-morrow, and to-morrow,
Creeps in this petty pace from day to day,
To the last syllable of recorded time;
And all our yesterdays have lighted fools
The way to dusty death. Out, out, brief candle!
Life's but a walking shadow; a poor player,
That struts and frets his hour upon the stage,
And then is heard no more: it is a tale
Told by an idiot, full of sound and fury,
Signifying nothing.
   —Act 5, Scene 5, 19-28

There is a long-held tradition among actors that one must never utter the name "Macbeth" outside an actual performance of the play—especially in a theater. Instead, one says "The Scottish Play." There is enormous superstition surrounding the tragedy, and perhaps I was one of its victims. I was twice cast to do Verdi's magnificent realization of Shakespeare's ill-fated King of Scotland, and both times I fell to its curse.

The first was a production with the New York Lyric Opera, early in my career. I was double-cast with another baritone. Few roles fit my voice as perfectly as Macbetto. The keys are perfect, the *tessitura* is ideal, and it's an actor's dream come true.

Rehearsals went beautifully, I was excited, and then—bang! I came down with a cold and laryngitis two days before the opening. With no chance of recovery, the other guy sang all the performances. I was shattered. All that work and anticipation for naught.

But things balanced out a few months later. The baritone scheduled to sing *Rigoletto* with the same company came down with a bug. I stepped in. But I'd already done *Rigoletto* and still regretted missing my chance to do the Scottish Play.

In 1987, more than fifteen years later, came another turn. I was offered the chance to do the role again at Portland Opera, where I had done *Pagliacci* with James McCracken a few years before. My voice was mature and lustrous, reaching its peak of perfection. It was my opportunity to correct a mischance of the past and have a success that could put me in the running for bigger things.

My hoarseness was recurring sporadically. I'd spent huge sums of money doctoring, with no clear treatment in sight. It was definitely asthma related, but there was something else, too. Nobody had a clue what it was. Still, applying a regime of steroids, vocal rest, and asthma medication, I had The Voice under control—most of the time. I had just finished *Pagliacci*, and though I had a reaction to some stage dust in the tech rehearsal, I was able to avoid any serious problems.

I relearned Verdi's masterpiece and carefully honed my voice for the upcoming production. It felt great, and I seemed to be managing well. And so I was—all the way through rehearsals. The Opera House in Portland, Oregon, is one of the most acoustically satisfying on the West Coast, and I looked forward to opening night like a giddy child anticipating Christmas. It was the first time I'd felt enthusiasm about my career in quite a while.

With me in this production were Pauline Tinsley, my old pal Gordon Greer, and another dear friend, Jerome Hines. Hines had done *Macbeth* with every great baritone since Leonard Warren, and this historical significance was not lost on me. Jerry was a monster of a man, a human redwood with a good heart and warm smile. He also was a Super Christian who would frequently tease me.

"What are you doing with a Jewish woman? You need to go out and find a good Christian girl."

I never had the heart to tell him I was an atheist. He purportedly owned an island somewhere, and I secretly wished for an invitation. So I kept my thoughts about organized religion to myself, as much out of respect for him as for my fantasy of some day basking in the waters around Jerry's island.

One day after rehearsal, unbidden, he said, "Charles, I've done this opera with all the greats, and you're as good as any of them, and better than quite a few."

I was speechless. Nothing, not love nor money, could have meant more to me than those words. Years of sacrifice, illness, and struggle had finally brought me the acknowledgment I sought.

Then the night of the dress rehearsal arrived. I stepped onstage for the first act.

"So foul and fair a day I have not seen..."

I saw stage fog all around me—a heated mixture of ethylene glycol, commonly known as antifreeze, and water. Moreover, I could smell it; it burned my lungs. It was like a nightmare.

No! I had been so careful, locking myself in my hotel room like a hermit, and now I was to be undone by this?

I sang the scene and, after leaving the stage, demanded that all the chemical fog be removed before I returned. They assured me it was the least caustic available, but it's so difficult to explain to others how tricky and unpredictable asthma can be. As a precaution, I marked—as we call it in the trade—conserving The Voice through most of the rehearsal for fear of irritating my cords. I occasionally tested it at full throttle, and it seemed okay.

After the rehearsal I went home, took a steaming shower,

and crossed my fingers. The next morning I was wheezing but thought I could get it under control. I had one more day of rest and didn't want to panic anybody at the company—and least of all myself—so I lay low and tried to stay calm.

On the morning of the performance, I awoke without a voice. My breathing was ragged and tight, and I could feel that my cords were not approximating. Singing produced only a thread-like, masked sound. I was in deep shit. I tried everything I knew to get it going but to no avail. I called Penny in a panic, and she boarded the next plane to Portland. I called the company, and all hell broke loose. There was nobody to cover me, and the performance could not be cancelled. I wasn't going to have another No Show on my conscience.

When Penny arrived, she put me in a cab and we went to the theater.

She said, "You're going to go out there and act it. Sing what you can, and speak what you can't."

In true actor's style, she reminded me, "The show *must* go on!"

Singing well feels like flying a kite. There's a wonderful, controlled tension between the wind, the kite, and the string in your hand. If all is well, you pull slightly on the string, and the kite rises and maneuvers with the slightest tug. Well, the sensation that night was like a kite plummeting to the ground. Air whistled through swollen vocal folds, and constricted bronchia produced a wheezy, thready sound.

I don't know what death feels like, but if there is a God, I pray to him that my last moments are less painful than the death of my career. I walked onstage, without a voice, to sing one of the greatest baritone roles ever written and, over the course of two hours, a part of me died, one agonizing phrase at a time. The culmination of a life's work evaporated like mist in a sunrise.

At the end of the show, I refused to take a curtain call, even though it had been announced to the audience that I was "indisposed." My colleagues came to my dressing room in turns to console the inconsolable. When all of the others had left, under cover of darkness, Penny and I skulked out of the theater. The next morning I was told they had engaged somebody else to do the next performance.

We went to the airport and flew back to Los Angeles.

I didn't speak or respond to anybody for weeks. I sat in my backyard, curled into myself, not interacting, just petting the dog and running the horror of the performance over and over again in my mind, wondering what I could have done differently.

Adrenaline plus obsessive thoughts.

It wasn't until after we had returned to L.A. that Penny told me about our friend Richard Levinson, the creator of such TV hits as "Mannix," "McCloud," "Columbo," and "Murder She Wrote." He had dropped dead of a heart attack the weekend of my opening.

Talk about Macbeth's curse!

"Maybe this will help you put your sorrow in perspective," she said.

Unfortunately, I could not balance the two tragedies. Sure, I hadn't died, but Richard was out of his misery. Mine was just beginning. Nonetheless, I tried to think philosophically and recognize that even remarkable success cannot guard you from the Grim Reaper.

A few months later, I tried one more time to overcome the inconsistency of my condition in a production of *Tosca* with Carol Neblett in Detroit. I hoped a success with a tried and true role, in a company where I had many good experiences, would erase the past. The last time I sang in Detroit, Louise had died, and I had no clue of the ironic symmetry that was about to be played out.

Tosca sealed my fate. I arrived hoarse and tried to work through it in rehearsal. One day I was clear. The next day it would return. I marked most of the rehearsals, thinking that if I could just ease my way in, I would be fine. Then my cords became inflamed during the dress rehearsal, and The Voice started to unravel. I went to see a doctor the next day, but he could only tell me what I already knew: There was no solution.

The day of the opera arrived, and I knew I was in trouble. I called the artistic director, and we decided that another NYCO colleague, Pablo Elvira, in town for *The Barber of Seville*, would sing from the side of the stage, using the score, while I acted the part. Herman Malamood and Ken Riegel came to mind.

I left town the next day. The baritone who had replaced me in *I Puritani* at NYCO flew in to do the rest of the performances. The vultures were circling. It was feeding time.

On the plane back to L.A., my mind wandered to the marvelous Italian baritone Ettore Bastianni. On being diagnosed with cancer of the throat, he decided that rather than have surgery and live without his voice, he would leave it untreated. He told almost no one of his illness and continued to sing, as crowds who once adored him booed his last performances. He died at age forty-four.

I swore I would never push my career past a point when I could no longer sing at my own high standards, so I personally called each company where I had future engagements and spoke to every director—many of whom were my friends—and cancelled my contracts.

I knew the harsh reality. Reliability was everything in this business, sometimes even more than talent. So much money was at stake each time a production was mounted that a singer with a questionable health problem, no matter how outstanding a performer, was a risk not worth taking. Even if they found a magic cure for asthma in the coming years, I could never rebuild what I had lost.

It was over. My dream was gone. I was grief stricken, but there was no other solution.

Postlude to a Scream: Perdition

A fish out of water writhes and gasps, agonizes, and finally dies. An artist removed from his creative dharma suffers no less, but unfortunately death does not come so soon. Instead, the artist must remain a lost soul in a purgatory between worlds, like a stroke victim who has lost the ability to communicate while clinging to the desperate desire to do so. A bird caged, a sea run dry, a volcano gone extinct—each a natural phenomenon whose purpose and potential is forever extinguished.

I sleepwalked through the months that followed, feeling neither pain nor pleasure, devoid of the capacity for rational thought, as the potion of adrenaline and obsessive thoughts burned the horrific sensations of humiliation into my DNA for eternity.

Arrogance wrought from talent quickly transforms itself to self-loathing when the gift no longer has expression. The deep-seated need to be remarkable flails about inside a claustrophobic crypt without windows or doors, and the only defense is to retreat into a kind of insanity.

My sleep was besieged by unspeakable nightmares, my waking hours by uncontrollable visions of disaster. My existentialism grew wings, mating with my mutated narcissism. I wished for some global catastrophe, thinking my only salvation rested in some radical change to life's ground rules. A pandemic, or a nice asteroid, would surely do the trick, something that could reset the calendar to zero—everywhere.

Penny, as optimistic as ever, trying to help in the best way she could, would sing that old Jerome Kern standard to me.

"Pick yourself up; dust yourself off, start all over again."

Then she'd respond to my unresponsive stares with animated pep talks about new beginnings and how crisis equaled opportunity. Though I realized she was acting out of love and concern, all it served to do was make me fantasize about pushing her in front of some fast-moving traffic on Olympic Boulevard.

Bit by bit, the incessant sighing subsided long enough for me to begin dabbling in some of my many hobbies. But even these diversions took on a subdued tone. I was drawn to ever-more dangerous activities, but the luck of the Irish was with me. No matter how hazardous my behavior, despite close calls, I walked away unscathed.

I had not amassed enough of a fortune to sustain me for the remainder of years my genetic propensity indicated I might live— certainly not in a fashion my retirement fantasies dictated. So when it appeared I would not have the untimely death I had been hoping for, I forced my mind toward some of the least objectionable options—something, as the Monty Python troupe used to say, "completely different."

I accepted the harsh reality that my musical career was over and assumed I would pursue some unrelated field. I was disillusioned beyond redemption and wished to abandon the Muse who had so treacherously deserted me at the apex of my productivity. I would, as my grandmother had so often observed, "cut off my nose to spite my face."

Yeah, right.

⤚ Epilogue

When you spend so many years perfecting the skills required to be a musician, the core of your being unrelentingly reminds you that it's unthinkable to simply walk away. But I tried.

Penny and I decided to leave California and strike off to the Pacific Northwest. I was convinced that the smog in L.A. had something to do with the onset of my asthma, so the fresh air of oxygen-producing forests sounded good. We bought a large, northwest contemporary house on an acre of land, complete with pond, on the outskirts of Redmond, Washington, the home of Microsoft and Nintendo. Actually, I should say Penny bought it. I was merely along for the ride, still nestled in a deep depression.

We dabbled in all sorts of things for awhile, even creating and teaching an elementary children's music method called "Kids and Keyboards."

Penny started a community orchestra and urged me to conduct. Working with amateurs was not something I was enthusiastic about, but nonetheless, on the eve on my fortieth birthday, baton in hand, I stepped before a rag-tag group of community players.

This continued for a couple of years, until we realized there was a vacuum for a medium-sized professional orchestra playing the repertory from Baroque through Mendelssohn. Soon thereafter, we formed Chaspen Foundation for the Arts, which sponsored our own professional chamber orchestra.

Despite my years of experience as a wind player, singer, pianist, and arranger, and weekly rehearsals with a community orchestra, the first time I stepped onto the podium before a group of professionals, I was petrified. But I used all my years of theatrical experience to hide it.

Penny was a dynamo of creativity, a one-woman band, so to speak. Bouncing back and forth between opera and theater most of her career, she had amassed a wide range of experience and skills that she put to good use. None of what happened would have been possible without her. She stood by my side while I was little more than a zombie. Amorously, intellectually, and musically we were inseparable. But that's another book—a screenplay, actually—so I'll leave it for now, other than to say that our partnership was the epicenter of all the creativity that defined the next decade.

Countless concerts followed, complete with a Summer Music Festival. Although these were marvelously productive years, the complexion of the Seattle music scene was changing. What had been a dearth of classical music in the area became a glut. Our product was good, but there were so many competing organizations that we were like an out-classed candidate running for office: We had a fresh message, wonderful ideas, and a visible track record, but we just couldn't raise enough money to remain in the race.

Eventually, we were pushing boulders uphill. The volunteer base was dwindling, money was drying up, and our hopes that the foundation would support us and our endeavors were evaporating. Despite our reputation we couldn't get over the hump. I blamed Penny's optimism, and she blamed my pessimism, which I, of course, felt was realism. Our life together was becoming darker than a Seattle sky in winter.

Despite the flurry of activity, some costly psychoanalysis, and a plethora of antidepressants, a deep, unsettling melancholy lay at the base of my every thought. There was no escaping it. Even though more than a decade had passed since I'd sung my last note, I remained broken-hearted, and each of life's disappointments and losses that followed were like weights tied to a drowning man's ankles. I sighed my way through the days, studying and plugging along until the next concert cycle began. Penny would take care of all the details then hand me the baton, and I'd conduct. Her initiative became my salvation. I barely functioned, except as reluctant musician and inattentive companion. I faced another potential defeat in both my professional and personal life and had no power to change it.

On Thanksgiving Eve 1999, the night before our second production of *Amahl and the Night Visitors*, Penny and I stood under the work lights on the stage of the Medenbauer Theater, painting sets. There was no one else to do it. It was cold and dusty, and the fumes from the paint burned my lungs. Penny was in Heaven. I was not. The music, which had always lifted me above life's uncertainties, just wasn't doing the trick.

After ten years, Chaspen Foundation was in an ever-spiraling vortex. But we plugged ahead and scheduled what were to be our last performances, which were artistically successful despite our crumbling relationship.

Two world-premiere operas, *The Ant and the Grasshopper* and *Twilight Voices*, signaled the sunset of my professional music career. Funding ceased. Penny and I began our own version of the movie *Mr. & Mrs. Smith* and, after nineteen years together, we split up a year later. She moved into a cabin in the woods, and I remained in the house. Life was never the same.

I began offering classes at a local college and taught privately. But once you've felt The Roar of the Greasepaint and the Smell of the Crowd, life quickly pales inside the drudgery of a normal existence. I craved the tingle of those regular adrenaline fixes one only gets from being on the stage in live performances, from illicit sex, or from life-threatening experiences.

One day, a few years later, after all the dogs had died, I found myself living alone in a house that had become a tomb flooded with memories. It was an albatross around my neck.

I closed the studio, sold the house, and liquidated everything I couldn't fit into my SUV. I drove to the Southwest, staying with friends, family, and a young woman who'd bounced in and out of my life like a ping-pong ball. Ours was an addictive, destructive relationship that shattered my last vestiges of trust in an entire gender of humanity. It left me so disillusioned I still wince at the contemplation of another relationship.

Ever since, I have roamed the country, following the sun, searching for something I can't quite put my finger on despite copious journaling and contemplation. I stay in one place for a while but inevitably move on, because in all my destinations no place feels like Home. I often fancy myself Ulysses chasing some great odyssey, or the Flying Dutchman, consigned to sail for eternity, coming ashore every seven years to seek someone to share his fate.

Still, my time is my own, and I don't fret much about the

future. I'm as graceful as a swan on roller blades, and though my hair is thinning and wrinkles are finding permanent residence on the topography of my face, my tan is deep, my smile infectious, and my laugh can still fill a room. My love of music has not faltered, and I still delight in learning a new song, despite a brief but inevitable angst that it will be a song unsung.

People I meet quiz me about my experiences with a National-Enquirer, curious-minds-want-to-know inquisitiveness, so a while back I started assembling notes and anecdotes. I'd always written and even had a number of articles published, so it seemed a natural step. And now, I've told my story—or some parts of it. If enough people find it compelling, I'll feel satisfied. If not, then perhaps I'll write something else.

The Road Taken

I once had a conversation with my mother about success. I talked about how I'd had the opportunity to sing at the highest level and realize so many of my dreams. To my surprise, she said, "Yes, but it didn't continue. So what did you really accomplish?"

Though I suspected there was no malicious intent in her rhetorical question, I was taken aback. But I realized she had a point. Under the judgment of society—which likes to measure, quantify, and pigeon-hole—my career was not an overwhelming success. I didn't get the gold watch, the fabulous wealth, or the place in operatic immortality I had dreamed of. Therefore my career, under those parameters, was a failure.

But, my God, what accomplishments I had along the way!

I did it my way, prevailed long enough to share the stage with some of the greats of my time, and was applauded as a celebrity in the international music scene. I met remarkable people, carried the torch for some of the most distinguished singers in history, and sang the music of the world's greatest composers. I conducted my own professional orchestra in thrilling performances and felt the exhilaration of leading highly talented musicians through countless compositions. I reached heights that most mortals can merely contemplate, only to fall like Lucifer to depths beyond my imagination.

Unfortunately, creativity is not an option. A compulsive desire at the core of creative people generates an indefinable energy toward being original and provocative. A need to express, through art, music, literature, dance, and drama, the profound emotions they experience. And though such emotions are not unique to them, artists are compelled to express theirs, naked before throngs of people. Beethoven struggled against deafness to compose some of the most sublime works in the annals of music because the desire was irresistible. Van Gogh and Emily Dickinson produced masterpieces in near-total obscurity their entire lives.

If a painter's hands become paralyzed, he will use his teeth. If a dancer loses her legs, she will choreograph. When a singer is robbed of his voice, he will pick up a baton, or write, perhaps. Our ability to create without a promise of remuneration is the easiest part.

Someone once asked about my writing, "So, you've been given an advance on your book, huh?"

"Nope."

"Has a publisher shown interest in the project?"

"Nope."

"You mean you sit for hours every day, writing with no guarantee of having it published?"

"Yep."

"Why?"

"I don't have a choice."

Postscript

Well, dear reader, as you may have guessed, things have changed. I met an old high school chum on Facebook, of all places, who runs a publishing company. He asked to see my manuscript and, a year later, on a promontory overlooking Uniontown, Pennsylvania, he told me he would love to publish it. It seems as though the world will get to read my narrative.

Meanwhile, I still wander through the western United States with the changing seasons, writing about my other great passions. You might see me in the press box at a big fight in Las Vegas or covering the Desert Classic Action Shooting Competition in Mesa, Arizona. Or, you might bump into me while hiking through one of America's national forests as I search for ammo brass, like a leprechaun struggling to remember where he stashed his pot of gold.

I still listen to music constantly, and I recently considered submitting my conductor's resume to a few opera companies. So, who knows? Life is full of opportunities for adventure. We only need the courage to reach out and grab them.

GLOSSARY

Andante con moto   A musical term indicating a moderate tempo, yet with movement. It comes from the verb *andare*—to go. Actually, *andare* can mean just about anything in Italian, from walk to run to drive.

Accelerando   Another musical term, meaning accelerating.

Acciaccatura   Literally meaning crushed or bruised, it refers to a short grace note typically notated with a slash through the stem or flag. Giuseppe Verdi (aka "Joe Green") used *acciaccaturas* extensively in Germont's aria "Di Provenzia Il Mar" in Act II of *La Traviata*. When sung, *acciaccaturas* sound a lot like hiccups.

Allegro Con Brio   A brisk tempo with some added brilliance and vigor.

Amahl and the Night Visitors   A one-act opera by American-Italian composer Gian Carlo Menotti. Commissioned by NBC and debuted on December 24, 1951, Amahl is sung by a boy-soprano—always a pain-in-the-ass to cast. Worse, these kids usually come with a Stage Mother. A Stage Wife is a bitch, but a Stage Mother is like a PMS-ing T. Rex.

Andrea Chénier   An opera in four acts by Umberto Giordano. Think *Les Misérables* on steroids. Madame Guillotine gets her prize.

Attila   An early Verdi opera about Attila the Hun. The libretto toys with history a bit by giving an Italian woman the credit for killing Attila. Quite a feminist feat in 453 AD. I wonder if she had to go to confession.

Blocking   A theatrical term synonymous with "staging." Blocking a scene involves setting the onstage logistics, including entrances and exits, as well as how, when, and where the actors/singers move. Most of this is done in a rehearsal room with tape on the floor to indicate scenery, before the cast has access to the set.

Bohème, La   An Italian opera in four acts by Giacomo Puccini. Four guys, who are not gay, inhabit the same loft in the Latin Quarter of Paris. (Although I always wondered about Colline. Any guy who thinks that much about the meaning of life is probably suspect.) Mimi, the girl upstairs, gets an itch in her britches and trundles down to the guys' loft to get a light for her candle (wink-wink), but the tenor is the only one home. They fall in love, she dies of consumption, and the characters all go back to their miserable lives.

Cadenza   Referring to the portion of a concerto or aria when the orchestra stops playing and the soloist plays/sings florid passages without strict or regular tempo. It provides an opportunity to show off virtuosity and, in some cases, improvisation.

Cantabile   In a singing fashion, songlike.

Cavalleria Rusticana   A one-act opera by Pietro Mascagni about the worst Easter Sunday you can imagine.

Corelli, Franco (April 8, 1921-October 29, 2003)   A tenor and one of the most remarkable specimens, both physically and vocally, in operatic history. He was renowned for his spectacular high notes and breathtaking good looks.

Covered, or *coperto* in Italian   In singing terms, the "covered voice" is the upper end of the male voice, which takes on a distinctly different sound due to the dropping of the larynx. The technique became common around the turn of the 19th century. Sometimes called *voce di petto* (voice from the chest), the term is misleading, because "covering" actually allows for more head voice, thus adding an upper extension to the range.

Don Giovanni   An opera in three acts by Wolfgang Amadeus Mozart and Lorenzo Da Ponte. It premiered in Prague on October 29, 1787. Purportedly, Mozart partied with the real Casanova in Prague before the opening. I'd like to have a video of that one.

Eugene Onegin   A dreary Russian opera by Pyotr Ilyich Tchaikovsky. The one shining moment is Lensky's Aria, "Kuda, kuda vï udalilis." Otherwise, good napping material.

Fanciulla del West, La   A quirky Puccini opera in three acts that takes place in a mining town in the Sierra Nevada Mountains of California during the 1840s Gold Rush. Jack Rance is my favorite role. I never needed to prepare. I simply played myself: cynical, misanthropic, irreparably damaged, and a great shot with a handgun.

Faust   A French opera in five acts by Charles Gounod based on Johann Wolfgang von Goethe's play. Long story short: An old guy sells his soul to the devil for another chance at youth. But he blows it; everybody dies and is either damned for eternity or saved by a choir of heavenly angels. Kind of like my last trip to Las Vegas.

Forza del Destino, La   An Italian work by Verdi that features two of the best duets for tenor and baritone in all of opera. It is a joy to sing.

Furioso all'isola di San Domingo, Il   An obscure opera by Gaetano Donizetti. Its plot is one of the most ridiculous, and the title role is so staggeringly difficult, that it's often referred to as Donizetti's *Lucia* for baritone. It also contains the only baritone duet I've ever encountered.

L'Amore dei Tre Rei   A long, convoluted opera by Italo Montemezzi with Strauss-like orchestration and Wagner-like ponderousness. Snore!

La brevità, gran pregio   Literally it means "brevity, great value." This is a line from the first act of *La Bohème* where, after burning Rodolfo's play to momentarily heat their freezing loft, Colline says, *Ma dura poco* ("But it lasted so briefly"), to which Rodolfo replies, *La brevità, gran pregio*. The figurative meaning is "in art, brevity is a desirable quality."

Lucia di Lammermoor   A Donizetti opera, in which an insane young girl living on the Scottish Moors with her psychopath brother murders her husband of an arranged marriage and has a mad scene with a flute *obbligato*. Lucia and the tenor die.

Manon Lescaut   A Puccini opera that, like Massenet's *Manon*, is based on the 1731 novel *L'histoire du chevalier des Grieux et de Manon Lescaut*. It's a tale of star-crossed lovers whose antics finally land them in the Louisiana wilderness, where Manon dies of starvation and exposure. What? Nobody knew how to fish?

Marito Disperato, Il   A dismal opera *buffa* (Italian comic opera) by Gennaro Cimarosa. If you ever get an offer to sing it—decline.

Marking   A term used mostly in singing and dance. To save voice/ strength during rehearsal, one "marks" to avoid fatigue. This means a dancer will leave out strenuous leaps or lifts while still maintaining the flow of the choreography. For singers, it usually means singing at a reduced volume and/or singing high notes an octave lower.

Mefistofele   An Italian opera by Arrigo Boito. It's the Italian version of *Faust*, more or less. The role of the Devil is sung by a bass in both. Why do basses have all the fun?

Mezzo-soprano   In opera, a medium soprano with a working range from A below middle C to the A two octaves above. However, Verdi requires the mezzo to go to B-flat with regularity and even C-flat (B natural) on occasion. For flings and offstage romances, give me a mezzo any day!

Molto Vivace   Very fast and vivacious. The tempo you use in anticipation of getting to the bar before it closes.

"…Muhammad Ali's chances of beating George Foreman for the heavy-weight title in Zaire."   Ali was on the comeback trail to the title after four years out of the ring because of his refusal to be drafted into the Armed Forces. He was not as fast as he was before his retirement, and Joe Frazier had knocked him on his ass in the 15th round of their bout at Madison Square Garden in March 1971. Two years later, George Foreman destroyed Frazier to win the title and easily KO'd Ken Norton, the man who had broken Ali's jaw the year before. Ali was not expected to get past the first round against Foreman in

the bout fought on October 30, 1974, in Kinshasa, Zaire. Some even feared for his life, but Ali won by knocking out Foreman in the eighth round in one of the greatest upsets in boxing history.

Pagliacci, I   A one-act opera by Ruggero Leoncavallo. It has one of the best arias for both tenor and baritone. Innumerable performances of Tonio paid for the sports car I owned in L.A. Booyah!

Pearl Fishers, The (aka *Les Pêcheurs de Perles*)   An opera in French by Georges Bizet. Believe me; you don't even want to know.

Padrone, Il   Master, owner, or manager, depending on the context. *Il Padrone di casa*, for example, means landlord or host.

Piu Grave   A musical term meaning very solemn.

Pinza, Ezio (May 18, 1892–May 9, 1957)   An Italian operatic basso who debuted the role of Emile De Beque in *South Pacific* on Broadway in 1949. He was supposed to be a real ladies man. Why *do* basses have all the fun?

Puritani, I   An opera by Vincenzo Bellini. Refer to *The Pearl Fishers* above.

Samson and Delilah   A French opera in three acts by Camille Saint-Saëns. The best thing about this opera is that it requires a throng of skimpily clad female dancers to portray all the hedonists. If you're lucky, you get to apply their body makeup.

Semi-demi-quaver   A note played for 1/32nd of the duration of a whole note.

Sextuplet   A group of six notes, or subdivisions, which fit within the duration of one beat.

Tosca   A Puccini opera in three acts. Taking place shortly after Napoleon's first Italian Campaign, it highlights the collision of three characters: an opera diva, a painter, and the Roman Chief of Police, a very nasty fellow. After lots of *Sturm und Drang*, everybody dies. The end.

The Tell-Tale Heart   A short story by Edgar Allen Poe. A tale of murder, insanity, and guilt. Poe at his best, if you like that sort of thing.

Three Days of the Condor   A political thriller directed by Sydney Pollack, in which Robert Redford plays a CIA analyst who gets to diddle Faye Dunaway at her hottest. Nuke the Arabs for oil? Why not?

Top of the voice   The upper singing range of the human voice.

Tozzi, Giorgio (January 8, 1923–May 30, 2011)   An American operatic basso. I'm not sure if he had any fun or not.

Trovatore, Il   An opera by Giuseppe Verdi with an unfathomable plot but some sensational music. Counts, troubadours, gypsies, maids, mischief, and misfortune (with a few nuns thrown in for good measure) make for a thrilling evening.

Welterweight   In professional boxing, a division in which the fighters may not exceed one-hundred forty-seven pounds. Known for its mix of power, speed, and stamina, I sometimes fantasized about fighting as a welterweight. But I know I would have gotten my ass pounded by even the lowliest among them. That's why I've stuck to writing about the sport.

Zaza   Composed by the same guy who wrote *Pagliacci*, it's an opera that's better heard than seen. The plot is replete with philandering ex-lovers and show business stereotypes. The baritone role of Cascart requires both forceful declamation and elegant lyricism. It's like Tonio and Silvio wrapped into one. The worst part is a child's speaking role in Act III. *Oy-vey!* The work is rarely mounted because it's a monster to produce. But if you like *Pagliacci* you'll *love Zaza*. Nobody dies!

ACKNOWLEDGMENTS

Thanks to my mother for all the expensive musical instruments and decades of lessons; to Aldo and Eileen DiTullio for their guidance and unrelenting optimism; to Louise for her belief in my talent; and to Penny for her affection, encouragement and all the early edits.

Thanks to William Goldman, whose book *Adventures in the Screen Trade: A Personal View of Hollywood and Screenwriting* inspired my title and structure; and to Michael Crichton, whose book *Travels* gave me the courage to write with fearless honesty.